Gourmet Bird Food Recipes

Cockatiel, Parrot, Budgie, Canary, Macaw, Cockatoo, Lorikeet, Amazon, Love Bird, African Grey, Lorie, Conures and others

Holly A. Armstrong
Michelle D. Bagnasco
Shannon R. Carbajal

BRISTOL PUBLISHING ENTERPRISES
SAN LEANDRO, CALIFORNIA

Printed in the United States of America.

ISBN: 1-55867-259-1

Cover design: Frank J. Paredes
Cover photography: John Benson
Illustrator: James Balkovek

CONTENTS

PREFACE

The parrot family (psittacines) includes many different types of birds. Large birds, such as cockatoos, cockatiels, macaws and African grays, and smaller birds, such as parakeets, budgerigars and love birds, all belong to the parrot family. The larger of these birds have a life span of about 80 years, which is very similar to a human's. The smaller birds live for 15 to 20 years. Just as with humans, the best way for parrots to live a full and happy life is to enjoy good nutrition.

Many people don't understand that birds have a sophisticated palate very much like humans. To aid in that understanding, and to provide recipes for foods that provide a variety of nutrition for our avian companions, we offer this collection. Two of us are vegetarians, and many of the recipes reflect that preference. If your household is not a vegetarian one, certainly offer meats, fish and poultry that you have cooked for your human family along with dishes found in these pages. Baby Bird loves a variety of nonvegetarian foods including hamburgers and chicken dishes (and seafood: a favorite is *Shrimp Citrus Salad*, page 104). You can also add fish, diced cooked meats and poultry to many of the dishes found in these pages.

These recipes have worked for many, many birds, but we do not know your bird, and the specific nutritional needs your bird may have. We recommend that you seek the advice of a good avian veterinarian about what foods he or she recommends. You can often find a good referral for an avian veterinarian at a reputable pet store.

The Joshua Foundation is a nonprofit foundation that provides sanctuary for abused or abandoned birds. Referrals are made to the foundation from the Humane Society, veterinarians, reputable bird dealers and other organizations and individuals who find birds needing assistance. Birds that can be rehabilitated are available for adoption, and birds unable to rehabilitate are given permanent shelter and care. The Joshua Foundation can be reached at 426 N. Wiget Lane, Walnut Creek, CA 94598, (925)-279-0781. The Joshua Foundation permanent care facility is located in Paradise, California, and can be reached at (530) 876 9100 or on the Foundation Website at www.joshua-foundation.com.

Holly A. Armstrong
Lafayette, California

Michelle Bagnasco
Concord, California

Shannon Carbajal
Paradise, California

A WELL-BALANCED DIET
FOR YOUR BIRD

No one knows exactly what a well-balanced diet for a bird is, but experts connected with avian research are coming closer to understanding the dietary requirements of the different species of parrots every day. We do know that every species is different, with different dietary needs, and those needs change with age and with the seasons (for example, during breeding and molting). Unlike their wild cousins, our pet birds are not able to forage for the proper foods. They depend on us. Until the experts can provide exact dietary guidelines as a result of their research, the best thing you can do is provide your bird with a variety of healthful foods.

Every bird will have likes and dislikes. You will need to experiment with a variety of foods and dishes to find new and exciting meals that will appeal to your bird. Give him, and the recipe, more than one chance. Try a rejected dish more than once. Sometimes an unfamiliar texture or taste takes awhile to get used to. Sometimes a bird will dislike a certain food for months — even years — and then one day it's his favorite! Keep offering everything.

Birds on an all-seed diet are not receiving proper nutrition. It can be very difficult to persuade a bird that is accustomed to eating only seeds to eat anything else. We suggest that you try everything and never give up. Your bird will benefit.

The feeding of pellet-type foods to birds is a science so new that no clear conclusions have been drawn. Our dedicated avian specialists will know more about this matter in the future. In the meantime, offer a variety of good food — pellets and seeds included — and work closely with your vet. Regular physical exams are a MUST for monitoring the health of your bird.

NUTRITIONAL TIPS

- Limit greasy, salty or high-sugar foods.
- Dark green vegetables are generally more nutritious than lighter ones.
- Acidic foods such as citrus fruits and tomatoes should be offered in small amounts only.
- Seeds high in protein include peanuts, hemp, caraway, safflower and flax.
- Seeds high in fat include rape, sunflower, flax, niger, hemp, poppy and peanuts.
- Seeds and grains high in carbohydrates include buckwheat, corn, millet, milo, wheat, oats and canary seed.
- Avoid altogether: alcohol, caffeine, avocados, rhubarb, tobacco, chocolate, apple seeds, and the pits of peaches, nectarines, cherries and avocados.

ABOUT VITAMINS

Use only vitamin supplements formulated especially for birds to add to your bird's diet.

Vitamin powders sprinkled in the drinking water dissipate only after a few hours. It is better to sprinkle the powder on a small amount of food that will be eaten right away: eggs, for example. Also, some vitamins dissolve readily in water and some do not. Some vitamins are fat-soluble. Examples of fat-soluble vitamins are A and D. Some other vitamins are destroyed by heat, so always wait for food to cool before adding vitamins.

VITAMIN D AND CALCIUM

The function of vitamin D is to transport calcium to the bloodstream. Calcium won't be absorbed without vitamin D. Your bird can manufacture his own vitamin D with the help of sunshine or full spectrum lighting (Vita Lights). There are also supplements available. If you choose a supplement, be careful not to give too much. Your bird can overdose on supplemental vitamin D, but he cannot overdose on sunshine.

Laying hens need extra calcium during the breeding season. African grays need extra calcium for their entire lives. Oats, such as oatmeal, sprouted oats and cooked whole oats, bind with calcium and take it out of the system. Oats are a good source of carbohydrates, but keep this in mind. Surprisingly, spinach has a chemical in it called oxalic acid, which also binds with calcium. Some spinach plants have been developed to eliminate the oxalic acid.

Two terms you should be aware of are *hyper* and *hypo*. Hyper means too much, and hypo means not enough. Two common examples are *hypervitaminosis* and *hypovitaminosis*.

Hypervitaminosis is a condition brought about by the absorption of too much of any vitamin. It is a condition that can cause aberrant behavior, such as feather-picking and "attitude" problems. Some of the vitamins that your bird can overdose on are D, E, C and A.

Hypovitaminosis, or not enough of a certain vitamin or vitamins, is more commonly observed than hypervitaminosis in the case of pet birds, especially not enough of vitamins A and D. But the use of supplements of these vitamins should be carefully monitored, as they are fat-soluble, which means that they are stored in the body. Again, too many supplements could result in hypervitaminosis. Consult your veterinarian about supplements and follow his advice.

Hypocalcemia is a lack of calcium. But remember, your bird can also overdose on calcium.

HELPFUL HINTS ABOUT FEEDING YOUR BIRD

Purchase supplies like cornmeal and flours at a health food store or a whole foods store. Refined cornmeal has little nutritional value and is prepared from sterile hybrid corn.

Some good substitute flours are millet, rice, soybean and whole wheat. These all have different textures, so if you are substituting any of these in a recipe, you might have to add more or less, depending on the flour.

Birds love warm food. Many of the recipes in this book are better served warm than cold. Make sure you test whatever you are serving, to make sure it is not too hot. Be especially careful about this if you are using a microwave oven. Stir to avoid hot spots.

Remember, your bird will benefit psychologically, as well as physically, from a wide variety of foods. Food is one of the best "playthings" you can give to your bird.

If you can get your bird accustomed to eating a certain kind of muffin (it doesn't matter what kind, but stick to the same kind for awhile), soon he will begin to recognize the shape and look forward to his muffin. Then you can begin to slowly sneak all sorts of ingredients into the muffins you bake for your bird. Pureed vegetables, wheat germ, nutritious flours, rice and crushed egg shell hide nicely in a muffin. Your bird will automatically sample it because of the shape.

PREPARING YOUR HOME (NEST) FOR LIFE WITH A BIRD

Nonstick cookware such as Teflon, Silverstone and T-Fal are very toxic to birds if overheated. They should be sold, or given to charity, and replaced with stainless steel, aluminum or cast iron.

All toxic material such as soaps, bleach, ammonia, insect poison and metal polish should be kept in a cupboard out of reach of your bird. As a rule, if a two-year-old child can get to it, so can a bird. However, if a lock or tie-down will keep out the two-year-old, it will not keep out a determined bird. Those not expert at safe-cracking are expert at knots.

If it is necessary to use toxic material such as oven cleaner, insect poison, ammonia, rug cleaner, paint, paint remover or paint thinner (to name only a few), remove the bird from the house and do not return it until the house is fully aired. This may be a good time to take your bird shopping or to the groomer for a birdie manicure. If the house is going to have a residual odor for some time (such as when painting), consider a long weekend camping or at the beach.

A happy bird has to live in a clean environment. In the wild, many of these birds live in the tops of trees; therefore their mess is dropped to the ground below, leaving them in a clean environment. Clean in and around the bird cage (the bird's room) with nontoxic cleaners. Simple Green is an excellent choice. It is not toxic to birds or the environment. White vinegar diluted in water is also an effective cleaning agent. Mild soap such as liquid Ivory is a good choice. Do not clean your bird's room with sprays if your bird is still in it.

Baby Bird (for more about the birds featured in this book, see the Table of Contents) prefers to have her room lined with the *London Financial Times*. She likes the color (pink), and when it is unfolded, it just fits her room. Jordie is less fussy, but does enjoy the Sunday comics. All birds should have their papers changed every evening. Two layers are put down so the top layer can be peeled off in the morning. Not only does this make the environment more sanitary for your bird, but — who knows — intellect could be enhanced with new reading materials twice a day! When the papers are changed, the room should be wiped down. Once a week, the room should be thoroughly scrubbed.

MULTIPLE PET HOUSEHOLDS

Birds are social animals, so they can form bonds with other family pets. Cats can often provide a bird with companionship and entertainment. To ensure a happy stress-free relationship among the pet family, the following should be considered.

Always be in attendance when your bird is out of the cage and there are other animals in the house.

Introduce a cat into the family when it is a very young kitten. Cats that are raised with birds seldom attack those birds.

Trim your cat's claws frequently. Cat scratches, even in play, can be fatal to a bird: a break in the skin can result in the development of pasteurella, a fatal bacterial infection.

Set boundaries. A large dog can critically injure a bird during a playful moment.

HOUSEHOLD DANGERS

- Adhesives used to repair, make models and glue surfaces have toxic fumes.
- Birds can drown in open toilets; small birds can drown in glasses of water.
- Cage wires that are too far apart can result in injury and strangulation.
- Be careful of ceiling fans — they can be fatal.
- Fumes from smoking can result in feather-picking or fatal respiratory infections.
- Partially open latches, frayed toy ropes, cracks between the wall and a piece of furniture, or other places where a bird could become stuck can result in fear that may lead to a heart attack.
- Gnawing on electric wiring can electrocute your bird.
- Nonstick surfaces on pots and pans and self-cleaning oven liners emit fumes that are toxic to your bird.
- Your bird's wings should be clipped to prevent flying into plate glass.
- Like small children, birds tend to put everything in their mouths, and can be poisoned from tin, verdigris, nicotine, mercury, lead, cleaning materials, insecticides, pencil lead (graphite), alcohol, coffee and avocados.
- Poisonous plants include oleander, acacia, yew, laburnum, viburnum, holly, dwarf elder, poinsettias and black honeysuckle.

- Birds hide illness. It is their way of surviving in the wild, as an ill or injured bird or animal is singled out as someone else's dinner. Therefore, observe your bird carefully for telltale signs.
- Before your bird is ill, find a reputable avian veterinarian. Local breeders, reputable pet stores and universities with a veterinarian program are good sources for referrals.
- Keep a record of your bird's weight. Loss of weight is the first sign of illness.
- Be attentive to changes in your bird's behavior and appearance.
- Cat scratches must be treated by your veterinarian immediately. The bacteria in a cat's claws and mouth are very toxic to birds.
- Inflamed eyelids and nostrils are a sign of a cold or respiratory infection.
- Salmonella infection can occur if fruit and vegetables are cut on a surface where raw meat has been prepared. It can also be contracted from unwashed egg shells.
- Moulting disorders such as insufficient new feathers or the appearance of brittle or broken feathers may be a sign of dietary deficiency. Supplement your bird's diet with animal protein and lots of fruit and green vegetables.
- Loss of coordination and/or equilibrium may be a sign of vitamin B deficiency. If not corrected, it can be fatal. Seek the care of a veterinarian, as vitamin B may

have to be injected into muscle tissue.

- Change in appearance of fecal matter is another important warning sign that something may be amiss with your bird. Seek the care of a vet in this case.
- Annual veterinary checkups are an excellent form of preventative medicine.

TRAVELING WITH YOUR BIRD: BABY BIRD'S TRAVEL CHECKLIST

Your bird may enjoy traveling as much as Baby Bird does (see page 37 for the story of Baby Bird). When Bill and Holly take off for their favorite destinations, the car or pick-up truck is loaded with Baby's paraphernalia. If they arrive without her favorite bowl or towel, she makes them deeply regret the oversight.

Bill and Holly find traveling with Baby adds a great dimension to any trip. Friends are made at rest stops. The world is viewed through a parrot's eyes. Surprises occur on every trip, such as recognizing MacDonalds and knowing she will share a hamburger; or having a stranger ask if she talks, to which she answers, "No."

Here is Baby's travel list, in her order of priority:

1. A bag of her favorite homemade granola (see page 116)
2. Her favorite blue bowl
3. Water dish
4. Current favorite knot toy

5. Travel perch
6. A large stack of towels (she uses inexpensive 100% pure cotton towels acquired from a warehouse club by the bale)
7. A bag of fruit-flavored, high-quality pellets
8. A bag of apples, carrots, green peppers and broccoli
9. A bag of unsalted roasted peanuts in the shell
10. A large bottle of water from home
11. A large ice chest for water and perishables
12. Travel carrier (Baby likes a medium-sized dog carrier that can be secured with a seat belt)
13. Emergency kit, including:
    - septic stick (to stop the bleeding from a broken feather, for example)
    - spray bottle for water for quick cool-down (if overheated)
    - antibiotic ointment
    - veterinarian's telephone number (always kept in wallet with driver's license)

JOSHUA'S STORY: THE BEGINNING OF THE JOSHUA FOUNDATION

It was a simple life. I was a research analyst for a major media company. My husband, due to an accident, was "Mr. Mom" to our 12- and 18-year-old sons, our 16-month-old cockatoo, Jasmine, and our gaggle of feisty cockatiels.

It seemed like a normal Saturday morning. My 18-year-old son, Billy, was rambling on about his date the night before. But instead of listening with only half an ear, this time I gave him my full attention. He was telling me about helping his girl friend babysit. He said the people had an African gray named Joshua in a mouse cage so small he couldn't turn around. He had no perch, and was required to hang upside-down like a little bat. He had spent 8 years of his 8½-year life in this "jail," with no toys or pastimes. He had an old chicken pot pie tin filled with black sunflower seed shells and a green pudding that was supposed to pass as water.

We had to buy Joshua to save him. The price was small, but at that point I would have mortgaged the house to do it. The story Billy told me could not have prepared me for what we found.

First, Josh had to be cut out of the mouse cage that encased his withered fragile body. He had no feathers except a small tuft on top of his head. His whole body was covered with thick wrinkled scar tissue, we assume from fire or electrocution. His wings were pinioned (partially amputated), a procedure that some sick countries, sick veterinarians and sick people still practice. The tendons in the back of his neck were cut so he could never lift his head higher than his shoulders, and he walked with a slow, painful gait. He was our little green wrinkled potato. His appearance was heart-wrenching, and his eyes, those beautiful, sorrowful, betrayed, come-help-me eyes, were the last thing I thought about as I closed my eyes and prayed at night, "Please help us to do right by Josh, amen."

This was the start of our new, wonderful, crazy, hectic, never-ending, fulfilling, rewarding, bang-your-head-against-the-wall life. We and Josh embarked on an exciting journey. He was the teacher, and we were the humble students.

We bought the biggest room made (we don't say cage). We wanted him to have enough room to do cartwheels. We got cotton perches for his sore feet and toys galore. We had a special manzanita tree made for him with thinner branches, close together.

Josh's muscles were so atrophied from lack of use and chronic confinement that he was unable to perch. Every time a sound was made, no matter how small, he would fall like a stone and smack his withered little body. We lined his room with down pillows covered with newspapers.

His appetite was wonderful. He ate anything and everything. Our vet said he would slow down, but for the time, his body was craving so many nutrients, every day was a smorgasbord. We had to make sure everything he ate was aiding his healing body.

The first few days were touch and go. We were told we should put him down. Never! Josh trusted us to pull him through. Today Josh is a beautiful, well-adjusted gentle soul.

Word spread throughout our tight-knit bird community, and soon we were getting calls from far and wide to ask for help and to get our permission to send us birds. Josh taught us about overcoming all odds and persevering through the darkest situations. I'm honored to carry his message through the Joshua Foundation (see more about the Joshua Foundation in Preface, page vi).

— Shannon R. Carbajal

BREADS AND PASTRIES

PERCHY PANCAKES

¾ cup flour
⅛ cup dry Cream of Wheat cereal
½ tbs. sugar
½ tsp. baking powder
¼ cup egg substitute
¾ cup milk
1 tbs. butter, melted
1-2 tbs. 100% fruit jelly spread

In a large bowl, mix together flour, cereal, sugar and baking powder. In a medium bowl, whisk together egg substitute, milk and butter. Add wet ingredients to flour mixture and stir to just moisten. Batter will be lumpy.

Heat a greased griddle or skillet over medium heat. Pour batter in scant ¼ cupfuls onto hot surface. Cook until bubbly, turn and cook until done. Spread with 100% fruit jelly. Makes 8 bird-sized pancakes.

CRESCENT FIX-UPS

1 tube (4 oz.) refrigerated crescent rolls (4 rolls)
½ cup shredded Monterey Jack cheese with jalapeños

Separate crescent roll dough into 4 triangles. Top each with 2 tbs. shredded cheese. Roll up and bake according to package directions.

ZUCCHINI CORN MUFFINS

1¼ cups flour
1 tbs. baking powder
¾ cup cornmeal
2 tsp. sugar
¼ cup buttermilk
3 tbs. vegetable oil
1 egg
12 oz. zucchini, shredded
2 oz. sharp cheddar cheese, grated

Heat oven to 425.° Coat 16 medium muffin cups with nonstick vegetable spray.

In a large bowl, combine flour, baking powder, cornmeal and sugar. In a separate bowl, combine buttermilk, oil and egg. Squeeze zucchini to remove most liquid. Add to dry ingredients with cheese. Pour in buttermilk mixture all at once and mix with a spoon just until evenly moistened.

Pour mixture into muffin cups and bake for 30 minutes or until browned on top and a toothpick inserted in the center comes out clean. Run a sharp knife around sides of muffins to remove. Cool on a wire rack. Makes 16.

SPICY SUCCOTASH MUFFINS

3 whole eggs with shells, washed
1½ cups cornmeal
½ cup flour
¼ cup corn oil
1 pkg. (10 oz.) frozen peas and carrots, defrosted
1 can (14¾ oz.) creamed corn
1 can (12 oz.) whole kernel corn (if fresh or frozen, use 1½ cups)
hot peppers and seeds to taste

Heat oven to 425.° Beat eggs and shells well and mix with remaining ingredients.

Grease two 12-cup muffin pans. Fill muffin cups about ½ full. Bake for 20 minutes or until a toothpick inserted in the center comes out clean. Run a sharp knife around sides of muffins to remove. Cool on a wire rack. Makes 24 muffins.

RAIN FOREST MINI-MUFFINS

2½ cups whole wheat flour
½ cup oat flour
¼ cup sugar
1½ tbs. baking powder
¼ cup chopped dates
¼ cup chopped peanuts
1 cup skim milk
¼ cup egg substitute
¼ cup vegetable oil
1 banana
1 cup chopped fresh cranberries, or ½ cup
    dried cranberries

Heat oven to 400.° In a large bowl, mix together flours, sugar, baking powder, dates and peanuts. Put milk, egg substitute, vegetable oil and banana in a blender container and process until banana is mashed. Add wet ingredients to dry ingredients and mix together quickly to form a stiff batter. If batter seems too wet, add more flour as needed. Fold in cranberries.

Grease two 12–cup muffin pans. Fill about ⅔ full and bake for 20 minutes or until a toothpick inserted in the center comes out clean. Makes 24 muffins.

BEAK-STICKING CORN MUFFINS

3 oz. cornmeal
¾ cup flour
1 tsp. baking powder
¼ tsp. salt
¼ cup water
¼ cup egg substitute
3 tbs. peanut butter
2 tbs. honey
½ cup skim milk

Heat oven to 425.° In a large bowl, mix together cornmeal, flour, baking powder and salt. In another bowl, mix together water, egg substitute, peanut butter, honey and milk until well blended. Pour wet ingredients into dry ingredients and stir just until moistened.

Spray 8 muffin cups with nonstick vegetable spray. Fill muffin cups and bake for 12 minutes, or until a toothpick inserted in the center comes out clean. Makes 8.

PAPAYA PUMPKIN SEED MUFFINS

½ cup diced dried papaya
¾ cup apple juice
2 medium eggs
2 tbs. olive oil
2 tbs. molasses
1 tbs. honey
2 tbs. wheat bran
1 cup sifted whole-wheat
   pastry flour
2 tbs. wheat germ
½ tsp. baking soda

1 tsp. baking powder
1 tsp. cinnamon
⅛ tsp. nutmeg
pinch ground ginger
½ cup pumpkin seeds

Soak papaya in apple juice for at least 1 hour or overnight. Drain papaya and reserve apple juice.

Heat oven to 400.° In a medium bowl, blend eggs, oil, molasses, honey, wheat bran and reserved apple juice. In a large bowl, mix together pastry flour, wheat germ, baking soda, baking powder and spices. Add wet ingredients to dry ingredients and mix until just well combined; do not over-mix. Stir in papaya and pumpkin seeds.

Line 12 muffin cups with baking cups or spray with nonstick vegetable spray. Spoon batter into muffin cups and bake for 12 to 15 minutes or until a toothpick inserted in the center comes out clean. Cool on a wire rack. Makes 12.

POTATO SUNFLOWER MUFFINS

½ cup sunflower seeds, shelled
1 tbs. butter or vegetable oil
1 cup corn kernels, fresh or frozen
2 cups mashed potatoes
2 eggs
¼ cup whole wheat pastry flour
½ cup wheat germ
¼ tsp. baking powder
½ tsp. pepper
¼ tsp. nutmeg
dash paprika

Heat oven to 400.° Sauté sunflower seeds in butter; add corn and stir well. In a large bowl, combine mashed potatoes, 1 egg and 1 egg white. Beat remaining egg yolk and reserve.

Combine pastry flour, wheat germ and baking powder and add to potatoes. Combine with potato mixture and add spices. Stir well.

Spray 12 muffin cups with nonstick vegetable spray. Spoon batter into cups and brush each muffin with egg yolk. Bake for 20 minutes or until golden brown and a toothpick inserted in the center comes out clean. Makes 12.

BIRDIE FRUIT AND VEGGIE MUFFINS

¾ cup cornmeal
¼ cup whole wheat flour
1 tsp. baking powder
¼ tsp. baking soda
¼ tsp. sugar
⅛ tsp. salt
2 tbs. nonfat dry milk powder
2 tbs. nonfat granola
1 tsp. wheat germ
1 egg, slightly beaten
⅛ cup grated carrots
1 jar (4 oz.) baby food vegetables
1 jar (4 oz.) baby food fruit
1 tbs. vegetable oil or margarine, melted

Heat oven to 400.° In a large bowl, mix together cornmeal, flour, baking powder, baking soda, sugar, salt, dry milk, granola and wheat germ. In a separate bowl, mix together egg, carrots, baby foods and oil. Add wet ingredients to dry ingredients and stir with a fork until moistened.

Spray 8 muffin cups with nonstick vegetable spray. Spoon batter into muffin cups. Bake for 15 to 17 minutes or until a toothpick inserted in the center comes out clean. Cool on a wire rack. Makes 8.

MUFFINS À LA MACAW

1¼ cups flour
½ cup instant Cream of Wheat
¼ cup sugar
1 tbs. baking powder
2 tsp. cinnamon
1 cup skim milk
¼ cup egg substitute
2 tbs. margarine, melted
1 tsp. vanilla extract
1 cup raisins
1 cup chopped nuts

Heat oven to 400.° In a medium bowl, combine flour, cereal, sugar, baking powder and cinnamon; set aside.

In a small bowl, combine milk, egg substitute, margarine and vanilla; stir into dry ingredients until just moistened. Stir in raisins and nuts.

Spoon mixture into 12 muffin cups. Bake for 18 to 20 minutes or until a toothpick inserted in the center comes out clean. Remove from pan and cool on a wire rack. Makes 12.

FLIGHT-WORTHY MUFFINS

5 tbs. (2¼ oz.) oatmeal
1 cup flour
2 tsp. baking powder
1 tsp. baking soda
½ cup raisins
2 eggs
3 tbs. honey
2 tbs. vegetable oil
1 cup plain low-fat yogurt

Heat oven to 350.° In a large bowl, mix together oatmeal, flour, baking powder, baking soda and raisins. In another bowl, mix together honey, oil and yogurt. Add wet ingredients to dry ingredients and stir until just moistened.

Spray two 12-cup muffin pans with nonstick vegetable spray. Fill muffin cups ⅔ full and bake for 15 to 20 minutes, or until a toothpick inserted in the center comes out clean. Makes 24 muffins.

JORDIE'S GRAHAM MUFFINS

¼ cup shortening
¼ cup honey
1 egg
1¼ cups all-purpose flour
¾ cup whole wheat flour
1 tbs. baking powder
½ tsp. salt
¾ cup milk

Heat oven to 400.° In a large bowl, cream shortening with honey. Add egg and beat well. In another bowl, sift flours with baking powder and salt. Add flour alternately with milk to shortening-egg mixture. Blend well.

Spray a 12-cup muffin pan with nonstick cooking spray. Fill muffin cups ⅔ full. Bake for 25 minutes, or until a toothpick inserted in the center comes out clean. Cool and freeze in air-tight containers, such as locking plastic sandwich bags. Makes 12.

APPLE BANANA DATE BREAD

1¼ cups flour
½ cup whole-wheat flour
2 tsp. baking powder
½ tsp. baking soda
½ cup chopped dates
1 cup applesauce
1 ripe banana, mashed, about ½ cup
½ cup honey
½ cup egg substitute
3 tbs. margarine, softened
2 medium apples, unpeeled and diced

Heat oven to 350.° Spray a 9-x-5-inch loaf pan with nonstick vegetable spray.

In a large bowl, combine flours, baking powder, baking soda and dates. In a medium bowl, beat together applesauce, banana, honey, egg substitute and margarine. Stir in diced apple. Combine fruit mixture with dry ingredients and spoon batter into loaf pan.

Bake in the center of oven for 60 minutes, or until a toothpick inserted in the center comes out clean. Remove to a wire rack and leave in pan for 10 minutes. Turn bread out onto wire rack to cool completely.

JORDIE'S CORNY HOT STICKS

1 cup cornmeal
1 cup flour
2 tbs. sugar
2 tsp. baking powder
3 tbs margarine, melted
1 small red bell pepper, chopped
1 small green bell pepper, chopped
1¼ cups buttermilk
¼ cup egg substitute
2 egg whites
½ cup corn kernels

Heat oven to 400.° Lightly coat a 9-inch square baking pan with nonstick vegetable spray. In a large bowl, combine cornmeal, flour, sugar and baking powder. Whisk gently to mix. In a large skillet, heat 1 tbs. of the margarine. Add red and green peppers and cook over medium heat until softened, about 3 minutes. Remove from heat.

In a medium bowl, mix together buttermilk, remaining 2 tbs. melted margarine, egg substitute and egg whites. Add cooked peppers and corn kernels. Pour into dry ingredients and stir until just combined.

Pour into prepared pan and spread to the edges. Bake for 30 to 35 minutes or until a toothpick inserted in the center comes out clean. Cool in pan. Cut into 12 pieces while still warm. Refrigerate leftovers in a sealed container. Serve warm. Makes 12.

COCKATOO CORNBREAD

4 eggs with shells, washed
½ cup broccoli florets
½ cup shredded carrots
1 green bell pepper, diced
2 pkg. (10 oz. each) frozen
   chopped spinach, drained
2 bananas
2 pkg. (8.5 oz. each) Jiffy cornbread mix
1 cup dry milk powder
16 oz. cheddar cheese, shredded

Heat oven to 350.° In a large bowl, beat eggs with shells. Add remaining ingredients and mix together well (tends to be soupy).

Spray a 9-x-13-inch baking dish with nonstick vegetable spray. Fill with batter and bake for 1½ hours, or until a knife inserted in the center comes out clean.

Cool and crumble into chunks sized appropriately for your bird. Arrange chunks one layer deep on cookie sheets and dry in a 200° oven until dry and crunchy. When cool, store in an airtight container. Keeps indefinitely.

MAJESTIC COCKATOO'S BIRD BREAD

10 fresh spinach leaves, washed
6 eggs, with shells, washed
3 carrots, shredded
4 cups water
2 cups whole wheat flour
3 cups cornmeal (white, self-rising)
2 cups multigrain cereal
1½ cups wheat germ
4 tsp. baking powder
2 tsp. baking soda
1⅓ cups dry milk powder
1 lb. peanut butter
2 tbs. molasses
2 cups applesauce
2 tbs. honey
1½ cups hulled millet seed

Heat oven to 300.° In a blender container, mix spinach, eggs, carrots and 2 cups of the water. In a large bowl, mix remaining ingredients. Add blended ingredients to bowl, adding remaining water as needed to moisten batter.

Lightly oil 3 bread pans. Spread mixture 1 to 1½ inches deep in pans.

Bake for 30 minutes or until brown. When cooled, cut into squares and freeze for later use.

BEAK-WATERING PUMPKIN BREAD

3½ cups flour
1 tsp. baking powder
2 tsp. baking soda
3 cups sugar
1 tsp. nutmeg
1 tsp. ground ginger
1 tsp. cinnamon
4 eggs
1 cup vegetable oil
2 cups pumpkin pie filling
⅔ cup orange juice
1 cup walnuts
1 cup raisins

Heat oven to 325.° In a large bowl, mix together flour, baking powder, baking soda, sugar and spices. In another bowl, beat eggs. Add oilk, pumpkin, orange juice, walnuts and raisins. Add wet ingredients to dry ingredients and mix well.

Grease and flour 3 bread pans. Fill pans ½ full with batter. Bake for 1 hour and 15 minutes or until a toothpick inserted in the center comes out clean. Cool loaves for 1 hour and slice while warm (not hot). Serve with butter.

FEATHER-RAISING FANTASTIC FRUITCAKE

1 cup whole wheat flour
¼ cup light brown sugar, packed
½ tsp. baking powder
¾ cup applesauce
¼ cup egg substitute
⅔ cup chopped dried apricots
⅔ cup dried pineapple chunks
⅔ cup chopped dates
½ cup raisins
½ cup chopped nuts

Heat oven to 325.° In a large bowl, combine flour, brown sugar and baking powder and stir to mix well. Add applesauce and egg substitute and mix well. Fold in fruits and nuts.

Coat two 5-x-3-inch loaf pans with cooking spray. Divide mixture evenly between pans and bake for about 45 minutes or until a toothpick inserted in the center comes out clean.

Remove bread and let sit for 10 minutes. Invert loaves onto a wire rack, turn right-side up and cool to room temperature. Wrap bread in foil and let sit overnight before slicing and serving.

FRUIT BARS WITH SEEDS AND NUTS

2 eggs
2 tbs. vegetable oil
1 tsp. vanilla extract
3 tbs. fruit juice
½ cup honey or molasses
⅓ cup whole wheat pastry flour
½ cup nonfat dry milk powder
½ cup wheat germ
¼ cup bran
1 cup raisins
¼ cup chopped dates or dried apricots
½ cup sunflower seeds
1 cup chopped nuts, any kind
½ cup sesame seeds

Heat oven to 300.° Beat eggs well and add oil, vanilla, fruit juice and honey. Stir in remaining ingredients. Batter will be thick and slightly sticky.

Spread batter into a well greased 9-inch square pan. Bake for 35 to 40 minutes or until firm. Cool on a wire rack and cut into squares.

AFRICAN OAT DELIGHTS

⅜ cup butter
⅛ cup honey
1 tsp. vanilla extract
1 egg, beaten
½ cup whole wheat flour
2 cups dry oatmeal
¾ tsp. baking powder
¼ cup sunflower seeds
1 tbs. water

Heat oven to 375.° In a large bowl, cream together butter and honey. Add vanilla and egg, beating in well. In another bowl, stir together flour, oatmeal, baking powder and sunflower seeds. Add dry ingredients to egg mixture and combine. Add water and stir until well blended.

Drop by teaspoonfuls onto a greased baking sheet and flatten slightly. Bake for about 10 minutes. Cool on a wire rack. Makes 2 dozen.

AVIAN GRAIN BAKE

½ cup wild rice
2 cups water
½ cup barley
½ cup bulgur wheat
½ cup steel-cut oats
1 tbs. butter
½ cup raisins
½ cup chopped pitted dates
6 cups water

Simmer wild rice in 2 cups water in a small saucepan for 20 minutes. Drain and set aside.

Heat oven to 375.° In a 2½-quart casserole dish, mix together barley, bulgur, oats, butter, raisins, dates, 6 cups water and cooked wild rice.

Cover loosely with foil and bake for about 1 hour, or until grains are tender and water is absorbed. Serve in ¼ cup servings. Serve warm. Refrigerate or freeze leftovers. Makes approximately 24 bird-sized servings.

CHEESE CRACKERS

1½ cups flour
¼ tsp. salt
¼ tsp. chili powder
½ cup butter, chilled
½ lb. sharp cheddar cheese, coarsely grated
2½ tbs. ice water

Mix flour, salt and chili powder in a shallow bowl. Cut in butter with a pastry blender until mixture resembles coarse meal. Add cheese and toss. Sprinkle ice water over surface 1 tablespoon at a time, mixing lightly with a fork. Dough should just hold together. Divide dough into 2 parts and turn out on a lightly floured board. Shape each into a roll about 9 inches long and 1 inch in diameter. Wrap in foil and chill well.

Heat oven to 375.° Slice chilled dough into rolls ½-inch thick and space 1 inch apart on an ungreased baking sheet. Bake for 10 minutes or until golden brown. Place on a wire rack to cool. Store in an airtight container.

NUTTY POLLY CRACKERS

1½ cups quick-cooking oats
½ cup flour
½ cup whole wheat flour
¼ cup wheat germ
¼ cup ground walnuts
1 tbs. sugar
⅔ cup water
¼ cup vegetable oil
2 tsp. water, divided
¼ tsp. red pepper flakes

Heat oven to 350.° In a large bowl, combine oats, flours, wheat germ, walnuts and sugar. Stir well. Add ⅔ cup water and vegetable oil, stirring until just moistened.

Divide dough in half. Roll each piece of dough into a 12-x-12-inch square on an ungreased cookie sheet. Cut each into thirty-six 2-x-2-inch squares. Brush dough with 2 tsp. water and sprinkle evenly with pepper flakes.

Bake for 25 minutes or until crisp and slightly brown. Separate crackers; remove from sheets and cool on wire racks. Store in an airtight container. Makes 6 dozen.

BUSY BEAK CHEESE TWISTS

¼ cup margarine or butter, softened
½ tsp. dried Italian seasoning, crushed
¼ tsp. garlic powder
1 loaf (16 oz.) frozen bread dough, thawed
½ cup grated Parmesan cheese
milk for brushing
1 tbs. sesame seed

In a bowl, stir together margarine, Italian seasoning and garlic powder. Set aside.

On a lightly floured surface, roll bread dough into a 12-inch square (if dough is too elastic, let rest 5 to 10 minutes). Spread margarine mixture evenly over dough. Sprinkle with cheese. Fold dough into thirds. With a sharp knife, cut dough crosswise into twenty-four ½-inch wide strips. Twist each strip twice and pinch ends to seal. Place twists about 2 inches apart on a greased baking sheet. Cover and chill for 6 to 24 hours.

Before serving: Heat oven to 375.° Brush a little milk over each twist. Sprinkle with sesame seed. Bake for 15 to 18 minutes or until golden. Makes 24.

BABY BIRD

Baby Bird is an Eleanora cockatoo. She shares her life with Bill and Holly Armstrong. Bill is a mineral consultant/rancher, and Holly is the managing partner of a Certified Public Accounting firm.

Baby goes to the office every day with Holly. She has become a CPA bird. Baby Bird spends her day on a special perch in Holly's office. She is generally very good. But about two or three times every day, she lets out a cockatoo war whoop. Clients not familiar with CPA birds think someone has been axed, or given a tax return with a startling balance due the IRS!

Baby named herself. Five years ago, when the Armstrongs were chosen by Baby to join her flock, her name was Rocky. After bringing her home, Holly said, "Isn't she the cutest baby bird?" From then on, if anyone said Rocky, she said, "Baby Bird." Since then, almost everything she says ends with *bird* — *fantastic bird, super bird, white bird, beautiful bird, your bird, tired bird*, and of course, *Baby Bird*. One time, when asked if she could talk, she said, "No, Baby Bird."

Baby shares her meals with the Armstrong "flock." Often, she is willing to share her food with the other members, and of course, she has to taste everything on anyone's plate.

Eleanoras are somewhere between a love sponge, a hyperactive child and a reserved, never-a-feather-ruffled princess. When Baby Bird is having a particularly hyperactive-child day, Holly has Baby do her exercises. Baby knows exercises require that she grip Holly's fingers with her claws and flap her wings while Holly raises and lowers her arm. Baby exercises until she is panting like a jogger, but not so out of breath that she can't still squawk. After a couple of bouts of exercise, Baby is read to calm down, groom her feathers and play with her favorite knot toy.

Baby loves her trips in the Armstrong truck or S.U.V. Whichever vehicle is taken, it is loaded to the ceiling with Baby's stuff (see *Traveling with Your Bird*, page 9). Bill and Holly are limited to sharing one small bag. On the 550-mile trip to the ranch, Baby has her favorite stopping places, including fast food restaurants and road-side rest stops. Each stop results in new friends and funny incidents, like playing in a drinking fountain — or the time Baby, Holly and Bill were thrown out of Denny's for having a bird, even in a bird carrier!

— Holly A. Armstrong

VEGETABLE AND FRUIT DISHES

VEGGIE CHIPS

8 oz. white potatoes
8 oz. sweet potatoes
8 oz. parsnips
8 oz. beets
red pepper flakes

Heat oven to 300.° Scrub unpeeled vegetables and cut into thin slices. Place slices in a single layer on a rack on a shallow baking sheet. Sprinkle lightly with red pepper flakes, if you like. Bake until crisp and lightly browned.

Baking times for each vegetable will vary. Start checking parsnip chips after 30 minutes. Potatoes need 40 to 50 minutes. Beets will take at least 50 to 60 minutes. Chips will soften slightly after a day due to humidity. To re-crisp, bake in 300° oven for 2 to 3 minutes.

RICO'S BEAN
AND SPROUT SALAD

¼ cup fresh bean sprouts
¼ cup steamed fresh green beans
1 tbs. chopped red bell pepper
2 tbs. sesame seeds
¼ tsp. red pepper flakes

Toss all ingredients together in a bowl. Serve as an appetizer or snack anytime.

BEAKY BIRD BEAN SALAD

½ cup fresh green bean pieces
½ cup fresh wax bean pieces
½ cup cooked kidney beans
1 stalk celery, diced
½ cup cooked black-eyed peas
½ cup cooked garbanzo beans
1 cup plain nonfat yogurt

Lightly steam fresh beans and combine with remaining ingredients in a bowl. This makes a complete meal for your bird.

BROCCOLI SOUFFLÉ

2 pkg. (10 oz. each) frozen chopped broccoli
½ cup chicken broth
2 cups well-drained cottage cheese
½ cup grated Parmesan cheese
2 eggs, beaten

Cook the broccoli in chicken broth and drain well. Combine cheeses and egg. Gently mix in broccoli. Bake in a greased 2½ quart casserole in a preheated 350° oven for 30 minutes or until a knife comes out clean.

ALMOND-TOPPED ZUCCHINI

3 tbs. margarine
⅓ cup slivered blanched
   almonds
6 medium zucchini

2 tbs. olive oil
¼ tsp. salt
⅛ tsp. pepper

In large skillet, melt 1 tbs. of the margarine over medium heat. Add almonds and cook, stirring frequently, until nuts are golden brown, about 6 minutes. Lift from pan with a slotted spoon and set aside. Cut each zucchini lengthwise into 6 sticks. Add remaining margarine and olive oil to skillet; add squash, salt and pepper. Cook over medium-high heat, turning frequently, until zucchini is tender-crisp when pierced with a fork, but not brown, about 12 to 14 minutes. Spoon into a serving dish and sprinkle with toasted almonds.

CHEESE ZUCCHINI

6 medium zucchini
garlic to taste
salt to taste
pepper to taste
pinch dried oregano
3 large ripe tomatoes
cheese slices

Heat oven to 350.° Quarter zucchini lengthwise and place in a shallow baking dish. Sprinkle with garlic, salt, pepper and oregano. Slice tomatoes and place over squash. Season again with a light sprinkle of herbs. Put a layer of cheese slices over tomatoes. Bake uncovered for 45 minutes.

ZUCCHINI SOUFFLÉ

2 lb. fresh zucchini
1 pkg. (8 oz.) cream cheese
salt and pepper to taste
buttered breadcrumbs

Slice and cook zucchini in salted water until tender. With an electric beater, beat cream cheese and zucchini until thoroughly mixed and fluffy. Season. Pour into casserole. Top with breadcrumbs and bake for 1 hour until top bubbles and/or cracks.

PASTA SALAD

For this recipe, you can add any fresh vegetables or use any zesty Italian dressing of your choice.

1 pkg. (10 oz.) garden rotini (3-colored
   twisted egg noodles)
1 cup broccoli florets
1 cup shredded zucchini
1 cup chopped celery
1 cup cut or shredded carrots
¼ cup chopped red bell pepper
1 can (2¼ oz.) sliced olives
½ cup sliced or shredded radishes
1 can (8.5 oz.) artichoke hearts, unmarinated,
   drained and cut into small pieces
1 bottle (16 oz.) Italian dressing

Cook pasta according to directions on package; drain. Toss vegetables with pasta. Add ½ of bottle of dressing. Toss again. Just before serving, add more dressing and toss again.

TOP RAMEN
SESAME SEED SALAD

2 pkg. (3 oz. each) chicken flavor Top
   Ramen noodles, crushed
¾ cup sesame seeds
½ cup slivered almonds
⅓ cup butter
½ head white or green cabbage, thinly sliced
½ head red cabbage, thinly sliced
Dressing, follows

Sauté noodles, seeds and almonds in butter until golden. Cool and add to cabbage. Add *Dressing* and toss to coat.

DRESSING

½ cup vegetable oil
¼ cup red wine vinegar
¼ cup sugar
2 tbs. soy sauce
1 flavor packet from Top Ramen noodles
salt and pepper to taste

Mix all ingredients together in a jar with lid and shake well to blend.

YUMMY DELICIOUS GREEN BEANS

2 cups fresh green beans
¼ cup slivered almonds
½ lemon
2 tbs. butter

Blanch green beans in boiling water for 5 minutes or less. Remove from pan and put green beans in ice water until chilled. Melt butter in a skillet. Add slivered almonds and sauté over medium-high heat until almonds start to brown. Add green beans. Squeeze lemon juice over beans. Continue to heat for about 3 minutes. Serve.

ZUCCHINI RICE CASSEROLE

1 cup rice
6 cups diced zucchini
1 cup grated Parmesan cheese
⅓ cup chopped fresh parsley
½ cup olive oil
pepper to taste
3 eggs, well beaten

Heat oven to 325.° Cook rice. Mix remaining ingredients with rice in a large bowl. Transfer to an ungreased 9-x-13-inch baking dish. Bake for about 45 minutes or until top is golden brown and bubbling.

SQUASH STIR-FRY

1 tbs. vegetable oil
1 small zucchini, cut into
⅟₄-inch slices
1 small yellow summer squash,
cut into ¼-inch slices
1 medium-sized red bell pepper,
cut into strips and halved
1 tsp. dried Italian seasoning, crushed
⅛ tsp. garlic salt

Heat a large skillet or wok over high heat and add oil. Add zucchini, yellow squash and red pepper strips. Cook and stir for 3 to 4 minutes or until vegetables are nearly crisp-tender. Add Italian seasoning and garlic salt; cook and stir for 1 minute more.

WINTER VEGETABLE
STIR-FRY

1 tbs. margarine or butter
1 medium turnip, cut into ½-inch cubes
1 medium-sized red bell pepper,
   cut into thin strips
1 medium-sized yellow bell peppers,
   cut into thin strips
1 medium-sized green bell pepper,
   cut into thin strips
1 medium carrot, cut into thin diagonal slices
2–3 tsp. lemon juice
¼ tsp. onion salt
⅛ tsp. pepper

In a large skillet or wok, melt margarine. Add turnip cubes. Cook and stir over medium-high heat for 2 minutes. Add red, yellow and green peppers and sliced carrot. Cook and stir for about 3 minutes more or until vegetables are crisp-tender. Stir in lemon juice, onion salt and pepper. Toss to coat.

BROCCOLI RICE CASSEROLE

1 pgk. (10 oz.) frozen broccoli spears
   or cut broccoli
1 cup quick-cooking rice
2 eggs, beaten
1½ cups shredded cheddar cheese
½ cup ricotta cheese
½ cup milk
½ tsp. dried marjoram, crushed

Cook frozen broccoli according to package directions. Drain and pat dry with paper towels. Prepare rice according to package directions.

Heat oven to 350.° In a medium bowl, stir together eggs, ½ cup of the cheddar cheese, ricotta cheese, milk and marjoram. Stir in rice. Pour into a lightly greased 10-inch quiche dish. Arrange broccoli on top. Sprinkle with remaining cheddar cheese.

Bake for about 20 minutes or until a knife inserted near the center comes out clean. Let stand for 5 minutes before serving.

BROCCOLI-CHEESE CASSEROLE

1 pkg. (10 oz.) frozen chopped broccoli
2 eggs, slightly beaten
1 cup dry cottage cheese
1 tbs. all-purpose flour
¼ tsp. dried thyme, crushed
⅛ tsp. pepper
1 cup shredded cheddar cheese

Place frozen broccoli in a 1-quart microwave-safe casserole. Microwave covered on 100% power (high) for 4 to 5 minutes or until broccoli is crisp-tender. Drain well.

Stir together eggs, cottage cheese, flour, thyme and pepper. Stir in cheddar cheese. Stir cheese mixture into broccoli. Microwave uncovered on high power for 4 to 6 minutes or until cheese mixture sets. Season with salt and pepper.

QUICK CORN SALAD

1 can (12 oz.) whole kernel corn
   with sweet peppers, drained
1 stalk celery, chopped
2 tbs. vegetable oil
1 tbs. sugar
1 tbs. cider vinegar
½ tsp. celery seed
¼ tsp. dry mustard
lettuce leaves

In a medium bowl, combine corn and celery. Make dressing: In a jar with a screw-top lid, combine oil, sugar, vinegar, celery seed and dry mustard. Cover and shake well. Pour dressing over corn mixture. Mix until coated. Line 4 salad plates with lettuce leaves. Spoon corn mixture on lettuce.

CAJUN CORN ON THE COB

4 ears frozen or fresh corn on the cob
3 tbs. margarine or butter
½ tsp. chili powder
¼ tsp. garlic powder
¼ tsp. cayenne pepper

Cook frozen corn according to package directions. Or, cook fresh corn covered in a small amount of boiling water for 6 to 8 minutes or until tender. Drain corn well.

In a small saucepan, melt margarine. Stir in chili powder, garlic powder and cayenne pepper. Cook over medium-low heat for 1 minute, stirring occasionally. Brush margarine mixture on corn and salt to taste.

BROCCOLI CORN BAKE

1 can (12 oz.) whole kernel corn, drained
1 cup frozen cut broccoli, loosely packed
⅛ tsp. pepper
4 oz. Swiss cheesc, in small pieces
2 tbs. milk
6 rich round crackers, such as Ritz,
   crushed (¼ cup)

In a 1-quart microwave-safe casserole, combine corn, broccoli and pepper. Microwave covered on high power for 3 to 4 minutes or until broccoli is almost tender. Stir in cheese and milk. Microwave covered on high power for 2 to 4 minutes or until cheese melts and broccoli is tender, stirring twice. Sprinkle crushed crackers on top.

CORN SOUFFLÉ

1 can (14¾ oz.) creamed corn
1 pkg. (8·5 oz.) Jiffy cornbread mix
1 can (12 oz.) whole kernel corn, drained
2 eggs, beaten
1 cup sour cream
½ cup margarine, melted

Heat oven to 350.° In a medium bowl, mix all ingredients together by hand. Spray an 8-inch glass baking dish with nonstick vegetable spray. Pour mixture into pan. Bake for 1 to 1½ hours, or until a toothpick inserted in the center comes out clean.

CHEESY SCALLOPED CORN

1 tbs. margarine or butter
8 shredded wheat wafers, crushed
1 can (12 oz.) whole kernel corn
   with sweet peppers, drained
½ cup shredded American cheese
¼ cup milk

Place margarine in a small microwave-safe bowl or custard cup. Microwave uncovered on 100% power (high) for 30 to 45 seconds or until melted. Toss with half of the crushed wafers. Set aside.

In a 1-quart microwave-safe casserole, combine remaining crushed wafers, corn, cheese and milk. Microwave uncovered on high power for 3 to 5 minutes or until cheese melts and mixture is heated through. Sprinkle with buttered wafers.

CHILLED CORN
AND RICE SALAD

1 pkg. (4.5 oz.) regular rice mix with mixed
    vegetables
1 can (7 oz.) whole kernel corn, drained
⅓ cup spices and herbs salad dressing
2 tbs. grated Parmesan cheese
lettuce leaves
grated Parmesan cheese for garnish, optional

Prepare rice mix according to package directions,
except start with hot water.

Place corn in a medium bowl. Stir in cooked rice mix.
Add salad dressing and 2 tbs. Parmesan cheese, stirring gently to coat well. Cover and chill for 3 to 24 hours.

Before serving, line a salad bowl with lettuce. Transfer
corn-rice mixture to salad bowl. Sprinkle with additional
grated Parmesan cheese, if desired.

BARLEY SALAD

1 cup hot water
¼ tsp. salt
⅔ cup quick-cooking barley
1 cup frozen small peas
1 small tomato, seeded and chopped
3 tbs. oil and vinegar salad dressing
1 tbs. lemon juice
¼ tsp. dried mint, dried basil, dried savory or dried
    chervil, crushed
lettuce leaves

In a small saucepan, combine hot water and salt. Bring to a boil and add barley. Return to a boil and reduce heat. Cover and simmer for 10 to 12 minutes or until barley is tender. Stir in frozen peas just until thawed. Drain and rinse barley and peas with cold water. Drain well.

In a medium bowl, combine barley mixture and chopped tomato. Add salad dressing, lemon juice and herbs. Toss lightly to coat. Cover and chill in the freezer for 10 minutes.

Line 4 to 6 salad plates with lettuce. Spoon barley mixture over lettuce.

DILLED TURNIPS AND CARROTS

1 lb. turnips, peeled and cut
　　into ¼-inch slices
2 medium carrots, thinly sliced
1 tbs. margarine or butter
1 tbs. all-purpose flour
1 tsp. dried dillweed
⅛ tsp. salt
dash pepper
⅔ cup milk
2 slices American cheese, 1 oz. each
⅓ cup plain croutons, crushed

Quarter turnip slices. In a medium saucepan, cook turnips and carrots covered in a small amount of boiling water for about 10 minutes or until tender. Drain well. Return vegetables to saucepan.

To make sauce: In a small saucepan, melt margarine. Stir in flour, dillweed, salt and pepper. Add milk. Cook and stir until thickened and bubbly. Cook and stir for 1 minute more. Tear cheese into pieces and add to sauce. Cook and stir until cheese melts.

Add sauce to turnips and carrots; gently stir together. Heat through. Transfer to a serving dish. Sprinkle crushed croutons over vegetables.

VEGETABLE KABOBS

1 small yellow summer squash,
   cut into 1-inch slices
1 zucchini, cut into 1-inch slices
1 small red bell pepper, cut into
   1-inch pieces
1 small green bell pepper, cut into
   1-inch pieces
1 can (16 oz.) whole white potatoes, drained
⅓ cup clear Italian salad dressing

In a medium saucepan, cook yellow squash slices, zucchini slices and pepper pieces in a small amount of boiling water for 1 to 2 minutes or until nearly tender. Drain well. Cool slightly.

To make kabobs: On 4 long skewers, alternately thread squash, pepper and potatoes, leaving a ¼-inch space between pieces.

Place kabobs on the unheated rack of a broiler pan. Brush kabobs with some of the salad dressing. Broil about 4 inches from heat for 3 minutes. Brush kabobs with more salad dressing, turn over and brush again with salad dressing. Broil for 3 to 5 minutes more or until vegetables are tender. Brush with remaining salad dressing before serving.

ZUCCHINI AND GREEN CHILES CASSEROLE

1½ lb. zucchini, sliced
4 eggs
½ cup milk
½ tsp. salt
½ tsp. pepper
3 tbs. flour
¼ cup chopped fresh parsley
1 can (4 oz.) chopped green chiles
½ lb. Monterey Jack cheese, grated
3 tbs. butter
grated Parmesan cheese

Heat oven to 350.° Cook zucchini in boiling water for about 2 minutes or until nearly tender; drain and cool. Mix eggs, milk, salt, pepper and flour. Add parsley, green chiles, cheese and zucchini. Pour into a buttered 9-inch square pan. Dot with butter and sprinkle with Parmesan cheese. Bake for 30 minutes.

MIXED FRUIT SALAD

4 cups shredded cabbage
1 can (17 oz.) chunky mixed fruit, drained
1 cup seedless red or green grapes
1 pkg. (3 oz.) cream cheese
3 tbs. orange juice

In a 1½-quart glass salad bowl, place 2 cups of the cabbage. Top with mixed fruit and grapes. Sprinkle with remaining cabbage.

To make dressing: In a small bowl, beat cream cheese until soft. Beat in orange juice.

Spread dressing over top of salad, sealing to edges of bowl. Cover and chill for 3 to 24 hours. Toss to serve.

FRUIT AND NUT SALAD

1 can (8¼ oz.) pineapple slices
1 tbs. lemon juice
1 medium banana, sliced
3 cups finely shredded cabbage
1 cup thinly sliced celery
1 can (11 oz.) Mandarin orange segments,
   drained
½ cup chopped walnuts
¼ cup raisins
1 carton (8 oz.) orange yogurt

Drain pineapple, reserving 2 tbs. syrup. Cut pineapple in chunks and set aside. Combine reserved syrup and lemon juice. Coat banana slices with 1 tbs. of the juice mixture and set remaining juice aside.

In a large bowl, combine pineapple, banana, cabbage, celery, oranges, nuts and raisins. Blend reserved juice mixture with yogurt. Add to cabbage mixture and toss lightly to coat. Cover and chill.

JORDIE

Jordie, an umbrella cockatoo, was one of the first rescues by the Joshua Foundation. While she was one of the more fortunate of the birds, in that she had suffered no physical abuse, she was abused due to the ignorance of her owners. Most people who adopt birds into their families don't understand the amount of time and love that birds require.

Jordie had been exclusively seed-fed (which is the equivalent of feeding a baby a diet consisting solely of chocolate cake), and every one of her wing feathers had been clipped, making it difficult for her to even glide from high points; thus she had no tail feathers from rough landings. In addition, her toenails had never been clipped and had grown back around into her feet, causing painful spurs. Fortunately, Jordie was rescued early enough that she suffered no psychological damage.

The first time I met Jordie, she was a pathetic-looking, dingy gray, scruffy bird who wanted nothing more than to spend hours clinging to my sweater, snuggling and getting "birdie loves." After several weeks of becoming comfortable in her new environment, Jordie came out of her shell and became *Birdzilla*. Silent as a shadow, she sneaks up, steals and disassembles pens in the blink of an eye and shreds houseplants, reducing them to nothing but dirt and roots, all the while saying, "Jordie, Jordie."

Jordie has an incredible personality. She loves to go shopping and meet new people, especially people wearing jewelry from which she can remove gems! She never walks, but rather hops like a kangaroo.

Jordie has become another CPA bird (read about Baby Bird, page 37). In our office we also have four parakeets that were rescued by the Joshua Foundation. They are not hand-trained, and spend all their time caged. When Jordie first discovered the "tots," she was obsessed by them. Every chance she got, she would run to their cage, scale it and watch them flutter madly about. After a time, the tots got used to her, and she no longer sent them into a frenzy, so Birdzilla had to come up with new ways of getting a reaction, including hanging upside-down from the side of their cage and screeching and flapping, and crawling underneath their seed tray and rocking their cage.

Jordie and the tots are now the best of friends. She shares her grapes with them, tells them, "Eat your grapes," and throws them toys like paper clips and disassembled pen parts that she steals.

— Michelle Bagnasco

POTATOES AND EGGS

MASHED POTATOES JORDIE-STYLE

2 tbs. dried potato flakes
2 tbs. hot water
2 tbs. milk
2 tbs. corn kernels, canned or frozen, thawed

Whip potatoes with hot water and milk. Stir in corn. Serve warm. Makes 1 bird serving.

FANCY BAKED FRIES

3 baking potatoes
¼ cup butter
2 tsp. anchovy paste
salt and pepper to taste

Heat oven to 350.° Scrub potatoes, but don't peel them. Cut potatoes so they resemble French fries, and spread them out on a baking sheet. Melt butter with anchovy paste and a dash of salt and pepper. Brush potato strips with anchovy butter and bake for 35 minutes.

GOURMET POTATOES

6 medium potatoes, unpeeled
2 tsp. salt
1 clove garlic, crushed
2 cups creamed cottage cheese
1 cup sour cream
½ pkg. (1 oz. pkg.) onion soup mix
½ cup shredded cheddar cheese
paprika to taste

Heat oven to 350.° Cook potatoes in boiling water for about 15 minutes, or until just tender. Cool. Peel and cut into small cubes. Sprinkle with some of the salt. Crush garlic in remaining salt. In a large bowl, combine cottage cheese, sour cream, onion soup mix and garlic-salt mixture. Fold in diced potatoes and pour into a 1½-quart casserole. Top with cheese. Bake for 40 to 45 minutes or until thoroughly heated and lightly brown on top. Sprinkle lightly with paprika.

SCANDINAVIAN POTATOES

8 medium potatoes
¼ cup butter
¼ cup grated Parmesan cheese
2 tbs. fine breadcrumbs
salt to taste

Heat oven to 425.° Peel, wash and pat dry potatoes. With a sharp knife, cut each potato into fairly thin slices almost all the way through. Potato should hold together and look like a small accordion. Melt 2 tbs. of the butter in a flameproof dish large enough to hold potatoes. Roll potatoes in butter until they are thoroughly coated. Sprinkle with salt and dot with remaining butter.

Bake for about 25 minutes, basting with butter. Sprinkle with cheese and breadcrumbs and bake without basting for 20 to 30 additional minutes or until tender.

VARIATION

Roll potatoes in butter and sprinkle with 3 to 5 tbs. dried herbs of your choice (parsley, chives, thyme or sage). Omit breadcrumbs. Substitute grated cheddar cheese for part of the Parmesan cheese.

RICO'S FAMOUS POTATOES

6 large russet potatoes
¼ cup butter, melted
1 can (14¾ oz.) cream of chicken soup
1 pint sour cream
½ cup grated cheddar cheese
¾ cup crushed cornflakes

Heat oven to 350.° Boil potatoes with skin on. Peel and grate potatoes with a large grater. Add melted butter and toss to coat.

In a separate bowl, mix together soup and sour cream. Transfer potatoes to a 9-x-13-inch ungreased baking dish. Add cheese and toss lightly with a fork. Pour soup mixture over potatoes and top with crushed cornflakes. Bake for 30 minutes.

OVEN-FRIED POTATOES

4 medium potatoes
¼ cup butter, melted
salt and pepper to taste
garlic to taste
paprika to taste
grated Parmesan cheese

Heat oven to 425.° Cut washed, unpeeled potatoes into slices about ⅛-inch thick. Spray a baking sheet with nonstick vegetable spray. Place potato slices on sheet in a single layer. Brush with melted butter. Add salt, pepper, garlic and paprika to taste. Bake for 15 to 20 minutes or until potatoes are crisp and golden. Sprinkle with Parmesan cheese after baking.

POTATO NACHOS

2 medium baking potatoes
1 can (4 oz.) diced green chiles, drained
1 can (9 oz.) nacho cheese dip
½ medium tomato, chopped

Heat oven to 425.° Scrub potatoes and trim ends. Cut potatoes into ⅜-inch-thick slices. Place slices in a single layer on a greased 12-inch pizza pan. Cover with foil. Bake for about 15 minutes or until just tender.

Spoon cheese dip over potatoes and sprinkle with green chile peppers. Bake uncovered for 3 to 5 minutes or until cheese is melted. Top with chopped tomato.

EASY CHEESY POTATOES

2 medium potatoes, about 5½ oz. each
⅓ cup water
½ jar (8 oz. jar) cheese spread with jalapeño peppers, about ⅓ cup

Scrub potatoes and cut into ¼-inch-thick slices. In a 1-quart microwave-safe casserole, combine potato slices and water. Microwave covered on high power for 5 to 7 minutes or until potatoes are just tender, stirring every 3 minutes.

Drain potato slices well. Cover with cheese spread. Microwave uncovered on high power for 30 to 60 seconds or until cheese melts. Stir melted cheese into potatoes.

ITALIAN HERBED POTATOES

2 green onions, sliced
1 tbs. margarine or butter
1 tsp. dried parsley flakes
¼ tsp. dried Italian seasoning, crushed
⅛ tsp. salt
3 cups frozen hash brown potatoes,
    loosely packed
¼ cup grated Parmesan cheese

In a 1-quart microwave-safe casserole, stir together green onions, margarine, parsley flakes, Italian seasoning and salt. Microwave covered on high power for 1½ to 2 minutes or until onion is tender. Stir in potatoes. Microwave covered on high power for 5 to 7 minutes or until heated through, stirring once. Add Parmesan cheese and toss to coat.

PARMESAN POTATOES

1 pkg. (7.6 oz.) instant mashed potatoes
    (enough for 4 servings)
¼ cup creamy Parmesan salad dressing
¼ cup shredded cheddar cheese

Prepare instant mashed potatoes according to package directions, except reduce water by ¼ cup.

Stir Parmesan salad dressing into hot potatoes. Sprinkle with shredded cheese.

FRENCH FRY CASSEROLE

1 medium-sized green bell pepper,
   chopped
3 tbs. margarine or butter
2 tbs. all-purpose flour
¼ tsp. pepper
1¼ cups milk
½ cup shredded American cheese
1 small carrot, shredded
1 tbs. diced pimiento
1 pkg. (20 oz.) frozen French fried
   crinkle-cut potatoes

To make sauce: In a large saucepan, cook green pepper in margarine until tender. Stir in flour and pepper. Add milk all at once. Cook and stir until thickened and bubbly. Cook and stir for 1 minute more.

Add ½ of the shredded cheese, shredded carrot and diced pimiento to saucepan, stirring until cheese melts. Stir French fried potatoes into sauce. Transfer to a 10-x-6-x-2-inch baking dish. Cover and chill for 3 to 24 hours.

Heat oven to 350.° Bake covered for 50 to 55 minutes or until potatoes are tender and mixture is heated through. Uncover and sprinkle with remaining shredded cheese. Bake uncovered for about 3 minutes more or until cheese melts.

CANDIED YAMS

3 cups water
3 large yams or sweet potatoes,
  peeled and thinly sliced
1½ tbs. vanilla extract
3 tbs. butter or margarine
2½ cups granulated sugar
2 cups brown sugar, packed
2 tbs. cinnamon
2 tbs. nutmeg

Heat oven to 350.° Into a 2-quart saucepan, put water, potatoes, vanilla and butter and cover with a tight-fitting lid. Bring to a boil, lower heat to medium and do not stir. Cook for 30 minutes. Add granulated sugar, brown sugar, cinnamon and nutmeg and replace lid. Continue to cook until water is lower and thickened. Check and if necessary, add more granulated sugar to taste.

Pour contents from saucepan into a 2-quart baking dish. Bake until lightly browned on top, about 20 minutes.

HONEYED
SWEET POTATOES

5 canned sweet potatoes
2 unpeeled oranges
salt and pepper to taste
2 tbs. butter
2 tbs. brown sugar
½ cup honey

Heat oven to 350.° Cut potatoes into 1–inch–thick slices. Cut unpeeled oranges into very thin slices. In a casserole dish, place a layer of sweet potatoes, a layer of orange slices, salt, pepper, dots of butter and sprinkles of brown sugar. Repeat with remaining ingredients. Pour honey over the top and bake uncovered for 45 minutes.

CINNAMON-SAUCED SWEET POTATOES

1 can (18 oz.) sweet potatoes, drained
2 tbs. brown sugar
2 tbs. apple or orange juice
1 tbs. margarine or butter
¼ tsp. cinnamon

Cut sweet potatoes into 1-inch-thick slices. Arrange potato slices in a 10-x-6-x-2-inch microwave-safe baking dish. Set aside.

In a 1-cup microwave-safe glass measure, combine brown sugar, apple juice, margarine and cinnamon. Microwave uncovered on 100% power (high) for 30 to 60 seconds or until mixture boils and margarine melts, stirring once. Pour cinnamon mixture over sweet potato slices. Cover with waxed paper. Microwave on high power for 3 to 4 minutes or until heated through.

HEARTY SCRAMBLED EGGS

1 cup frozen hash brown potatoes
   with onions and peppers,
   loosely packed
¼ tsp. pepper
⅛ tsp. ground sage
2 tbs. margarine or butter
8 eggs
⅓ cup milk

In a large skillet, cook hash brown potatoes, pepper and sage in margarine over medium-high heat for 2 minutes. Reduce heat to medium. Cook for about 3 minutes more or until potatoes are tender, stirring occasionally.

In a medium bowl, beat together eggs and milk. Add egg mixture to potato mixture in skillet and stir.

Cook without stirring until egg mixture begins to set on the bottom and around the edges. Use a large spoon or spatula to lift and fold partially cooked egg mixture so uncooked portions flow underneath. Continue cooking over medium heat for about 4 minutes or until eggs are cooked through but are still glossy and moist. Serve immediately.

SAVORY EGGS

1 cup grated American or cheddar cheese
2 tbs. butter or margarine
½ cup light cream
½ tsp. salt
¼ tsp. pepper
1 tsp. prepared mustard
6 eggs, slightly beaten

Heat oven to 325.° Spread cheese in a greased 9-x-13-x-2-inch baking dish. Dot with butter. Combine cream, salt, pepper and mustard. Pour ½ of the cream mixture over cheese. Pour beaten eggs evenly over cheese and cream. Add remaining cream mixture. Bake until set, about 30 minutes.

If desired, prepare the night before and refrigerate; bake the next day.

CRUSTLESS QUICHE

1 pkg. (10 oz.) frozen cut broccoli
3 eggs
1 can (5 oz.) evaporated milk
1 jar (5 oz.) Old English cheese spread
¼ cup all-purpose flour
1 tsp. Worcestershire sauce
½ tsp. dry mustard
¼ tsp. pepper

Heat oven to 400.° Generously grease bottom and sides of a 9-inch pie plate. Set dish aside.

Place frozen broccoli in a colander. Run hot water over broccoli just until thawed. Drain well. Layer broccoli in prepared dish.

In a blender container or food processor workbowl, combine eggs, evaporated milk, cheese spread, flour, Worcestershire sauce, dry mustard and pepper. Cover and blend for about 15 seconds or until well combined. Pour egg mixture over broccoli in prepared dish.

Bake for about 20 minutes or until a knife inserted near the center comes out clean. Let stand for 5 minutes before serving.

EGG AND CHEESE PUFFS

1 can (7½ oz.) semicondensed savory cream
   of mushroom soup
1 cup milk
⅛ tsp. pepper
2 cups shredded cheddar cheese
4 eggs, separated
⅛ tsp. cream of tartar

In a medium saucepan, stir together soup, milk and pepper. Cook and stir until bubbly. Add cheese; cook and stir until melted. Stir ½ of the hot soup mixture into beaten egg yolks. Return soup-egg yolk mixture to the saucepan. Cook and stir for 2 minutes more.

In a large bowl, with an electric mixer, beat egg whites and cream of tartar until stiff peaks form (tips stand straight). Fold soup mixture into egg white mixture. Spoon mixture into six 6-ounce custard cups. Seal, label and freeze for up to 1 month.

Before serving: Heat oven to 300.° Remove custard cups from freezer and thaw for 2 hours. Set custard cups in a 9-x-13-inch baking pan. Pour boiling water into pan around cups to a depth of ½-inch. Bake for 50 to 55 minutes or until a knife inserted near the center comes out clean. Serve immediately.

CHEESE EGG CASSEROLE

3 eggs, beaten
½ cup milk
¼ cup all-purpose flour
¼-½ tsp. dried basil, crushed
¼ tsp. baking powder
¼ tsp. salt
¼ tsp. pepper
2 cups shredded mozzarella cheese
¾ cup cream-style cottage cheese
1½ oz. cream cheese, cut into pieces
4 green onions, sliced
1 medium tomato, chopped

Heat oven to 350.° In a bowl, beat together eggs, milk, flour, basil, baking powder, salt and pepper. Add mozzarella cheese, cottage cheese and cream cheese pieces and beat until well combined. Stir in green onions.

Pour egg mixture into a well-greased 9-inch pie plate. Bake uncovered for 25 to 30 minutes or until mixture is set in the center. Sprinkle chopped tomato around the edges. Let stand for 5 to 10 minutes before serving.

EGG AND POTATO BAKE

3 medium potatoes, cooked and sliced
3 eggs, hard–cooked and thinly sliced
2 tbs. butter
1 cup milk
dash Worcestershire sauce
1 tsp. salt
pepper to taste
1 cup grated cheddar cheese
raw wheat germ
2 tbs. flour

Heat oven to 350.° In a saucepan over medium heat, melt butter, stir in flour, add milk and cook slowly, stirring until thickened. Add Worcestershire sauce to taste and salt and pepper. Stir in grated cheese.

In an oiled 1½-quart casserole, layer ½ of the sliced potatoes, ½ of the eggs and ½ of the cheese sauce. Repeat. Sprinkle with wheat germ and bake for 20 minutes.

RIGALETTO
(OR RICKI WITH AN "I")

Josh was on his way to fantastic recovery when our flock began to expand (see page 11 for the story of Josh).

Rigo, short for Rigaletto, a triton cockatoo, was bought when he was 3 months old by an American family living in Malaysia. He was the center of attention. He lived in the kitchen where all of the family congregated.

Life was great for Rigo. Taunting the maid in three languages, playing toss with the children, tormenting the dogs — basically the normal life of a cockatoo. The family had to move to the United States for business reasons, and of course Rigo, being a family member, moved with them. He did his tour of duty in the necessary quarantine stations and fared pretty well. The next year or so life was pretty much the same as it was in Malaysia. Sweet, lazy days — a bird couldn't ask for more. But when Rigo's family had to move back to Malaysia, they didn't want him to go through the quarantine process again, so they didn't take him.

Rigo found his way to an exclusive bird store where he performed his antics. I went in from time to time and laughed at this comedian who did a wonderful Stevie Wonder, performed somersaults, played catch and chattered nonstop. His encore was a wings-out, feathers-on-end, glass-shattering scream — crowd-pleasing, but not the act of a take-home birdie that anyone wanted. Slowly Rigo stopped talking, the performances became fewer, and he started chewing his chest feathers and losing weight.

On one of my visits I looked for the crazy clown, and didn't see him. When I asked, I was directed to the back of the store where a once vibrant, happy bird was now a shaking, drawn wreck, basically dying of a broken heart.

Rigo went home with me that night. We squeezed three birds, three trees and three "bird rooms" into our bedroom. It was a tight fit, but we were a family. We mixed love with a proper diet (we really had to put on the Ritz to get him to eat) and a lot of laughter, and soon our Rigo was back to his old self.

Except that it was *her* old self! We have now found out Rigo is really Ricki, a female bird. She's going through the terrible twos, and life is never dull! She loves entertaining the handicapped and children who are ill. She keeps them laughing, and just as it worked with Ricki, laughter and love are the best medicine!

— Shannon R. Carbajal

ENTRÉES AND SIDE DISHES FOR YOU AND YOUR BIRD

MACARONI AND CHEESE

2 tbs. butter
4 tsp. flour
1 cup skim milk
½ cup grated cheddar cheese
¾ cup cooked macaroni
chopped broccoli or green bell pepper,
  optional

In a large saucepan over medium heat, melt butter, add flour and cook for 1 minute. Add milk and cook until mixture thickens. Add cheese and cook, stirring until melted. Add macaroni and stir to coat. For variety, add chopped broccoli or peppers.

MACARONI, CHEESE AND PEAS

1 pkg. (about 7 oz.) macaroni and cheese mix
½ cup buttermilk salad dressing
¼ tsp. pepper.
1 cup frozen peas
¼ cup milk, optional

Prepare macaroni and cheese according to package directions. Stir in salad dressing and pepper. Fold in peas. Chill in the refrigerator for 3 to 24 hours, if desired. Stir in milk to moisten if necessary.

CHEESY LITE
BAKED MACARONI

4½ oz. dried macaroni
2 cups cooked broccoli
6 oz. low-fat cheddar cheese
4 oz. skim mozzarella cheese
2 tbs. wheat germ
½ tsp. salt
1 cup evaporated skimmed milk

Heat oven to 450.° In a large pot of boiling water, cook macaroni according to package directions until tender. Drain. Return to same pot and combine with broccoli, cheeses, wheat germ and salt. Spoon into a 6-cup baking dish and pour milk evenly over the top. Bake for 15 minutes, until golden and bubbly.

VEGGIE-NOODLE TOSS

3 tbs. water
1 tbs. vegetable oil
¼ tsp. garlic powder
1 tsp. red pepper flakes
1 pkg. (3 oz.) ramen noodle soup
1 green bell pepper, cut into thin slices
2 cups pea pods
1 cup fresh bean sprouts
1 cup shredded carrots
1 cup fresh broccoli florets
1 pkg. (10 oz.) frozen corn
1 cup fresh cauliflower florets

In a jar with a screw-top lid, combine water, oil, garlic powder and red pepper flakes to make dressing; shake and set aside.

In a medium bowl, break up ramen noodles; discard seasoning packet. Pour enough boiling water over noodles to cover. Set aside for 1 minute, and then drain. In large bowl, combine noodles and all vegetables. Add previously prepared dressing and toss to coat. Cover and refrigerate. Serve cold.

FARFALLE À LA MARCELLO SILI

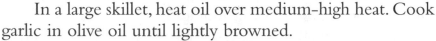

3 tbs. olive oil
3 cloves garlic, finely chopped
1 lb. assorted vegetables,
   cut into bite-size pieces
pinch salt and pepper
¾ cup chicken broth
2 tbs. mascarpone cheese or cream cheese, softened
pinch dried oregano leaves
1 lb. bow tie pasta, cooked according to package
   directions and drained
grated Parmesan cheese

In a large skillet, heat oil over medium-high heat. Cook garlic in olive oil until lightly browned.

Add vegetables, salt and pepper and cook, stirring frequently, until vegetables are crisp-tender. Add broth, mascarpone and oregano and toss to combine. Toss freshly cooked pasta with vegetable mixture. Serve with grated Parmesan cheese.

ROTELLE AND CHEESY VEGETABLES

1 pkg. (4 oz.) rotelle
2 cups coarsely shredded
   cabbage
2 cups sliced carrots
1 cup water
2 stalks celery, sliced
½ medium-sized green bell
   pepper, chopped
3 tbs. butter or margarine
3 tbs. all-purpose flour
2 tsp. instant chicken
   bouillon granules

1 cup shredded mozzarella
   cheese
1 cup shredded fontina cheese
¼ cup grated Parmesan
   cheese
⅓ cup toasted wheat germ
¼ cup fine dry
   breadcrumbs
¼ cup chopped walnuts
2 tbs. butter or margarine,
   melted

In a large saucepan, cook rotelle in boiling salted water until tender. Rinse with cold water and drain. Set aside.

In the same saucepan, cook cabbage and carrots in water for about 10 minutes or until nearly tender. Drain well, reserving liquid. Add enough water to reserved liquid to measure 1 cup total liquid. Set liquid and vegetables aside.

In the same saucepan, cook celery and green pepper in 3 tbs. butter until tender but not brown. Stir in flour and bouillon granules. Add reserved 1 cup liquid. Cook and stir until mixture is thickened and bubbly. Cook and stir for 1 minute more. Add cheeses, stirring until melted. Gently stir in rotelle, cabbage and carrots.

Heat oven to 375.° Turn vegetable mixture into a greased 1½-quart casserole. Stir together wheat germ, breadcrumbs, walnuts and 2 tbs. melted butter; sprinkle over vegetable mixture. Bake for 20 to 25 minutes or until hot and bubbly. Let stand for 10 minutes before serving.

TORTELLINI IN CREAM SAUCE

1½ cups frozen broccoli, cauliflower and carrots
1 pkg. (7 oz.) frozen cheese-filled tortellini
¾ cup hot water
½ tsp. minced garlic, or ⅛ tsp. garlic powder
¼ tsp. dried marjoram, crushed
⅛ tsp. pepper
½ cup whipping cream
¼ cup grated Parmesan cheese

In a large skillet, combine vegetables, frozen tortellini, water, garlic, marjoram and pepper. Bring to a boil. Reduce heat, cover and simmer for 7 minutes. Drain well. Stir in cream and Parmesan cheese and heat through.

TORTELLINI AND VEGETABLES

1 pkg. (7 oz.) cheese-filled tortellini
1 pkg. (16 oz.) frozen broccoli, cauliflower
   and carrots
1¼ cups milk
½ pkg. (1.8 oz. pkg.) white sauce mix, about
   3 tbs.
6 oz. creamy Havarti cheese, cubed

Cook tortellini according to package directions, adding frozen vegetables the last 5 minutes of cooking. Drain.

To make sauce: In a small saucepan, heat milk until warm. Stir in white sauce mix. Bring to a boil, reduce heat and cook and stir for 1 minute. Remove from heat. Add cheese, stirring until melted.

Pour sauce over tortellini-vegetable mixture. Toss lightly and serve immediately.

GARLIC-BUTTERED VERMICELLI

6 cups hot water
6 oz. vermicelli
1 tbs. margarine or butter
1 tsp. minced garlic, or ¼ tsp. garlic
   powder
1 tbs. snipped fresh parsley
grated Parmesan cheese

In a large saucepan, bring water to a boil. Add vermicelli, reduce heat slightly and cook in gently boiling water for 5 to 7 minutes or until tender. Drain in a colander.

In the same saucepan, melt margarine. Stir in garlic. Add vermicelli and parsley and toss to coat. Transfer to a serving bowl. Sprinkle with Parmesan cheese.

PARMESAN NOODLES AND CARROTS

1½ cups hot water
½ cup milk
2 tbs. margarine or butter
1 pkg. (4.5 oz.) noodles
   with Italian cheese sauce
1 cup frozen crinkle-cut carrots
grated Parmesan cheese

In a medium saucepan, combine hot water, milk and margarine. Bring to a boil and stir in noodle mix and carrots. Return to a boil and cook uncovered for about 8 minutes or until noodles and carrots are tender, stirring occasionally. Transfer to a serving bowl. Sprinkle with Parmesan cheese and serve immediately.

PASTA AND ASPARAGUS TOSS

6 cups hot water
4 oz. spaghetti, broken into 3-inch pieces
1 pkg. (10 oz.) frozen cut asparagus
⅓ cup dairy sour cream
2 tbs. brown or Dijon-style mustard
⅛ tsp. pepper
1 small tomato, chopped

In a large saucepan, bring water to a boil. Add spaghetti. Reduce heat slightly and cook in gently boiling water for 8 minutes.

Break up frozen asparagus before removing it from the package. Add asparagus to spaghetti in the saucepan. Return to boil, reduce heat and cook for about 4 minutes more or until spaghetti and asparagus are just tender.

Drain spaghetti and asparagus in a colander. Place colander in a large bowl of ice water. Let stand for 5 minutes. Drain well.

In a small bowl, stir together sour cream, mustard and pepper. Transfer drained pasta and asparagus to a serving bowl. Add sour cream mixture and tomato and toss lightly to coat.

CHILES STUFFED WITH RICE

1 cup cooked rice
½ cup grated Monterey Jack cheese
2 tbs. sour cream
1-2 cans (7 oz. each) whole green chiles

Heat oven to 400.° Combine rice, cheese and sour cream. Split and remove membrane and seeds from chiles. Fill with rice mixture. Place filled chiles in a greased 10-x-6-x-2-inch or 8-inch square baking dish. Cover with foil. Bake for 15 to 20 minutes.

CHEESE SOUFFLÉ WITH CHILES

8 eggs, separated
1½ tsp. flour
¼ tsp. salt
¼ tsp. pepper
2 cans (4 oz. each) whole green chiles, washed
   and seeded
2 cups shredded Monterey Jack cheese

Heat oven to 350.° Beat egg whites until stiff. Mix flour, salt, pepper and egg yolks. Fold in beaten egg whites and pour ½ of this mixture into a greased 2-quart baking dish. Spread chiles over egg batter and cover with shredded cheese. Pour remaining egg mixture over cheese. Bake for 30 minutes.

GREEN CHILES
AND CHEESE BAKE

1 tbs. butter, softened
8 slices thickly sliced bread
3 oz. sharp cheddar cheese, shredded
3 oz. Monterey Jack cheese, shredded
1 cup milk
1 can (4 oz.) whole green chiles,
    drained and cut into strips
3 large eggs

Heat oven to 350.° Butter 4 slices of bread and place bread buttered-side down in an 8-inch square baking dish. Sprinkle chiles and cheeses over bread slices and top with 4 remaining bread slices.

Beat eggs and milk, stirring to blend, and pour over bread. Bake for 40 minutes or until brown.

BAKED CHEESE OMELETS

¼ cup butter
1 cup finely diced cooked ham,
    about ¼ lb.
6 eggs
½ tsp. salt
few dashes hot pepper sauce
½ tsp. rubbed sage
¼ tsp. dried thyme
¼ tsp. dried tarragon, crushed
¼ cup flour
½ tsp. baking powder
1 cup small curd cottage cheese
2 cups grated Monterey Jack cheese

Heat oven to 400.° Melt butter in a skillet. Spoon 1 tsp. melted butter into each of 4 individual baking dishes (¾ to 1 cup each). Coat dishes with butter. Add ham to remaining butter in skillet and sauté for about 5 minutes over medium heat.

In a medium bowl, beat eggs with salt, hot pepper sauce, sage, thyme, tarragon, flour and baking powder. Mix in cheeses and ham. Spoon into baking dishes, distributing ham as evenly as possible. Bake for 15 minutes. Set oven heat to 325° and bake for 15 minutes longer or until puffed and golden.

QUICHE À LA AVIAN

½ cup butter
8 eggs, separated
2½ cups ground ham with no fat
generous ½ cup grated Swiss cheese
1 cup cream
salt and pepper to taste
⅔ cup plain breadcrumbs

Heat oven to 350.° In a large bowl, cream butter. Add egg yolks and beat well. Add ham, cheese, cream, salt and pepper. Beat egg whites until stiff and lightly fold into ham and cheese mixture. Lightly mix in breadcrumbs. Recheck seasoning.

Spread evenly in a greased 9-x-13-inch glass dish. Bake for 20 minutes. This recipe can be baked the day before and warmed to serve.

DILLED VEGGIE PIZZA

2 tubes (8 rolls each) refrigerated
   crescent rolls
1 pkg. (16 oz.) frozen broccoli,
   cauliflower and carrots
1 cup milk
½ pkg. (1.8 oz. pkg.) white sauce mix,
   about 3 tbs.
8 oz. creamy Havarti cheese, shredded
1 tbs. dried dillweed

Heat oven to 375.° Unroll dough and separate into 8 rectangles. Arrange rectangles in an ungreased 15-x-10-x-1-inch baking pan. Press over bottom and up sides of pan to form a crust. Seal perforations. Bake for 14 to 16 minutes or until golden.

Place frozen vegetables in a colander. Run hot water over vegetables just until thawed. Drain well. Cut up any large pieces.

To make sauce: In a small saucepan, heat milk until warm. Stir in white sauce mix and bring to a boil. Reduce heat and cook and stir for 1 minute. Remove from heat. Add 1 cup of the cheese and dillweed, stirring until cheese melts.

Spread sauce over baked crust. Top with vegetables. Sprinkle with remaining cheese. Bake for about 5 minutes more or until heated through.

CURRIED RICE

1 can (14½ oz.) chicken broth
⅓ cup raisins
1 tbs. curry powder
1 tbs. margarine or butter
1½ cups quick-cooking rice
⅓ cup coarsely chopped peanuts

In a medium saucepan, combine chicken broth, raisins, curry powder and margarine. Bring to a boil and stir in rice. Cover and remove from heat. Let stand for about 5 minutes or until liquid is absorbed. Stir and sprinkle with chopped peanuts before serving.

SPANISH RICE SKILLET

1 cup mild salsa
1 cup quick-cooking rice
1 small green bell pepper, coarsely chopped
1 can (8 oz.) whole kernel corn, drained
½ cup hot water
½ cup shredded cheddar cheese

In a medium skillet, stir together salsa, green pepper and water. Bring to a boil and stir in rice and drained corn. Sprinkle with cheese. Cover and remove from heat. Let stand for 5 minutes before serving.

PILAF-STYLE RICE

1 cup hot water
1 cup frozen peas
1 pkg. (1 oz.) instant onion soup mix
1 tbs. margarine or butter
1 cup quick-cooking ricc
1 tbs. diced pimiento

In a medium saucepan, combine hot water, frozen peas, soup mix and margarine. Bring to a boil and stir in rice. Cover and remove from heat. Let stand for 5 minutes. Stir in pimiento and serve.

BEANS, RICE AND SPINACH BAKE

1 cup dry pinto beans, cooked after measured
1 cup dry brown rice, cooked after measured
½ cup shredded cheese, or more
1 lb. fresh spinach, steamed
2 eggs, beaten
1 cup milk

Heat oven to 350.° Combine cooked beans, cooked rice, cheese and steamed spinach in a 2½-quart casserole.

In a small bowl, mix eggs and milk and pour over rice mixture. Stir gently and bake for about 45 minutes.

ITALIAN TORTELLINI SALAD

6 cups hot water
1 pkg. (7 oz.) cheese-filled tortellini
4 oz. provolone or mozzarella cheese,
  cubed
1 small tomato, coarsely chopped
½ small yellow or green bell pepper, cut
  into thin strips
½ cup Italian salad dressing
¼ cup grated Parmesan cheese

In a large saucepan, bring 6 cups hot water to a boil. Add tortellini. Reduce heat slightly and cook in gently boiling water for about 10 minutes or until tender.

Drain tortellini in a colander. Place colander in a large bowl of ice water. Let stand for 5 minutes. Drain well.

Transfer chilled tortellini to a serving bowl. Add cubed provolone or mozzarella cheese, tomato and pepper strips. Pour dressing over tortellini mixture. Toss gently to coat. Add Parmesan cheese and toss lightly.

CHICKEN AND RICE SALAD

1 cup chicken broth
¼ tsp. dried dillweed
1 cup quick-cooking rice
2 cans (5 oz. each) chunk-style chicken,
    drained and broken into large pieces
1 cup seedless red grapes, halved
½ small cucumber, seeded and chopped
⅓ cup mayonnaise or salad dressing
⅓ cup sour cream
milk for thinning

In a medium saucepan, combine broth and dillweed. Bring to a boil and stir in rice. Remove from heat. Let stand, covered, for 5 minutes.

Stir chicken, grapes, cucumber, mayonnaise and sour cream into rice mixture. Transfer to a bowl; cover and refrigerate for 3 to 24 hours.

Before serving, thin chicken mixture, if desired, by stirring in milk, 1 tbs. at a time, to desired consistency.

ITALIAN-STYLE COUSCOUS SALAD

1 medium zucchini, cut into ¼-inch slices
1 can (14½ oz.) tomato wedges, drained
2 medium carrots, shredded
1 cup quick-cooking couscous
⅓ cup clear or creamy Italian salad dressing
2 tbs. water

In a large bowl, combine zucchini, tomato wedges, carrots and uncooked couscous. Stir together Italian salad dressing and water. Drizzle over couscous mixture. Toss gently to coat. Cover and chill for 3 to 24 hours.

BEAN SALAD

4 cans (16 oz. each) beans: garbanzo beans, wax beans,
    green beans, kidney beans or pinto beans
½ cup chopped celery
½ cup red and green bell pepper strips
¾ cup white wine vinegar
¾ cup dark brown sugar
½ cup vegetable oil

Rinse and drain all beans and combine with celery and peppers in a large bowl. In a small saucepan over high heat, bring wine vinegar, brown sugar and oil to a boil. Pour hot dressing over bean mixture and toss to coat. Refrigerate for 24 hours. Drain dressing and reserve if desired. Serve plain or on lettuce.

SHRIMP CITRUS SALAD

2 medium-sized ruby grapefruit
2 large stalks celery, diced
1 lb. cooked, shelled tiny shrimp
Lime Marinade, follows
salt and pepper
1 can (4 oz.) water chestnuts
1 head butter or iceberg lettuce

With a sharp knife, cut skin and white membrane from grapefruit. Hold fruit over a bowl and cut segments free. Squeeze juice from membrane into bowl; discard membrane.

Drain grapefruit juice into another bowl and add celery, shrimp, *Lime Marinade* and salt and pepper to taste. Cover grapefruit bowl and shrimp-celery bowl and chill both for at least 1 hour or overnight.

Dice water chestnuts and stir into shrimp mixture. Arrange a bed of lettuce on each of 4 salad plates. Set aside a generous tablespoon of the shrimp mixture and 1 grapefruit segment for your bird. Spoon remaining shrimp mixture on each bed of lettuce and arrange grapefruit segments over salads. Spoon marinade over salads.

LIME MARINADE
⅓ cup lime juice
2 tbs. ketchup
1 tbs. vegetable oil
1 tbs. white vinegar

2 finely chopped green
   onions, ends trimmed
1 tsp. dry mustard

Stir ingredients together.

FLEMISH POT ROAST

1 beef chuck roast, 4-5 lb.
1 tbs. vegetable oil
4 medium onions, sliced
2 tbs. butter or margarine
2 tbs. flour
1 can (12 oz.) beer
1 tbs. brown sugar
1 tbs. red wine vinegar
1 bay leaf
2 cloves garlic
1½ tsp. salt
2 tbs. minced fresh parsley
hot mashed potatoes

In a heavy Dutch oven, brown meat in oil, turning to brown both sides. In a separate pan, sauté onions in butter until pale golden.

Sprinkle with flour and cook for 2 minutes. Pour in beer and bring to a boil, stirring. Pour onion mixture over meat. Add brown sugar, vinegar, bay leaf, garlic and salt. Cover and simmer for 2 hours or until meat is tender.

Transfer meat to a hot platter and sprinkle with parsley; keep warm. Reduce pan juices with onions until juices are slightly thickened. Strain juices into a sauce bowl. Spoon onion into a vegetable bowl. Carve meat. Pass gravy and onions at the table. Serve with mashed potatoes.

HONEY CHICKEN

2 tbs. sesame seed
3 tbs. honey
¼ cup dry sherry or dry white wine
¼ cup Dijon mustard
1 tbs. lemon juice
6 boneless, skinless chicken breast halves,
   about 8 oz. each
salt and pepper
steamed white rice

Heat oven to 400.° Heat a 10- to 12-inch skillet over medium-high heat and add sesame seed; stir until light brown. Pour seed into a small bowl and add honey, dry sherry, mustard and lemon juice; stir to blend thoroughly.

Arrange chicken pieces slightly apart in a 9-x-13-inch baking dish or pan and spread evenly with honey-sesame seed mixture. Bake uncovered until breasts are no longer pink in the thickest part (cut to test), 15 to 20 minutes. Baste several times with honey mixture while baking.

With a slotted spoon, transfer chicken to a warm platter or plates and bird bowl; pour sauce into a small bowl and offer it with each portion. Serve with steamed white rice.

BABY'S FAVORITE CHICKEN

This is actually Baby's favorite meal, period!

enough chicken legs and thighs
   for the whole flock
olive oil
rosemary
pepper

Heat oven to 375.° Rub legs and thighs with a mixture of olive oil, rosemary and pepper to taste. Bake in an oven-proof casserole for 45 minutes or until meat is loose from the bone. Remove most of the meat from 2 leg bones (leave knuckle and some meat attached) and cool before serving. Serve with baked potatoes and a cucumber salad. The human flock is allowed to share the leftovers.

CHICKEN NUT BITES

1 cup chicken broth
½ cup butter or margarine
1 cup all-purpose flour
1 tbs. chopped fresh parsley
2 tsp. seasoned salt
2 tsp. Worcestershire sauce
¾ tsp. celery seed
½ tsp. paprika
⅛ tsp. cayenne pepper
4 eggs
1 can (5 oz.) boned chicken, drained and
  chopped
¼ cup chopped toasted almonds

Heat oven to 400.° In saucepan, combine chicken broth and butter. Bring to a boil. Stir in flour, parsley, seasoned salt, Worcestershire sauce, celery seed, paprika and cayenne. Cook, beating rapidly, until mixture leaves sides of pan and forms a smooth compact ball. Remove from heat.

Add eggs, one at a time, beating well after each addition, until mixture is shiny. Stir in chicken and almonds. Drop by rounded teaspoons onto ungreased baking sheets. Bake for 15 to 18 minutes or until browned. Serve hot. Makes 75 bites.

HARLEY
THE GENTLE GIANT

Harley is a harlequin macaw (a green wing cross with blue and gold). We think Harley is about 10 years old.

Harley spent most of his life as a status symbol for a drug dealer. He existed in an ornamental cage with no toys, no light and little positive human contact. He usually had a bowl of peanuts and slimy water. He grew up in a methamphetamine laboratory inhaling drugs, and was fed beer, alcohol and marijuana. He hung on the side of his cage and screamed for attention. In return, he was beaten on the feet with a cane — his toes were either crushed or beaten until they fell off. He was poked with sticks and stun guns, and had his beautiful tail set on fire.

Harley's owners were finally arrested. He was passed from person to person, until we were told that the current owner would sell him. Of course, we bought him. By this time, we had converted part of our home to an aviary.

Harley had a solid brick wall around his heart so thick it would take years of love and trust to penetrate it. We chip away a little each day. His diet needed a lot of attention. He was no underweight, because he had been fed dry cereal, Twinkies, peanuts and sunflower seed by the pound. He was used to candy, chips and beer. It was hard to compete with that, and to convert him to food that is nutritious and good-tasting. Finally Harley is slimming down nicely and is becoming a sweet, kind big bird. Like the other birds rescued by the Joshua Foundation, he will never again feel pain and neglect — only love and care.

— Shannon R. Carbajal

TREATS

BUSY BEAK BALLS

1 cup peanut butter
⅓ cup dry milk powder
¼ cup raisins
¼ cup graham cracker crumbs
¼ cup toasted sesame seeds
½ cup coconut
¼ cup honey

Mix ingredients together, saving some of the coconut. Roll into balls, and roll balls in remaining coconut to coat. Chill thoroughly and store in a cool place.

PARROT PARTY MIX

¼ cup butter
½ tsp. chili powder
1 cup mixed shelled nuts
1 cup cooked garbanzo beans, not mushy, well drained

Heat oven to 400.° Melt butter and combine with chili powder. Place nuts and garbanzos in a large bowl and add butter mix. Stir until well coated and turn out into a shallow baking pan. Bake for 15 to 20 minutes, stirring once or twice.

BIRDIE BARS

2 eggs with shells, washed
2 tbs. vegetable oil
1 tsp. vanilla extract
3 tbs. fruit juice, any kind
1 cup raisins
¼ cup chopped dates or apricots
½ cup honey or molasses
½ cup nonfat dry milk powder
½ cup wheat germ
⅓ cup whole wheat pastry flour
¼ cup bran
1 cup chopped nuts
½ cup sunflower seeds
½ cup sesame seeds

Heat oven to 300.° In a large bowl, beat eggs with shells. Add oil, vanilla and fruit juice. Stir in remaining ingredients. Batter will be thick and sticky. Spread batter in a well-greased 9-inch square pan. Bake for 35 to 40 minutes or until firm. Cool and cut into squares.

PARROT'S PARADISE

½ lb. dates
1 lb. dried figs
1 cup peanuts
1 lb. dried apricots
½ cup raisins
1 tsp. sesame seeds

Chop dates, figs, peanuts, apricots and raisins finely with a food processor. Spoon out by teaspoonfuls and shape into small balls. Roll in sesame seeds. Refrigerate any leftovers.

PERKY PARROT PEANUT PATTIES

2 cups whole
   wheat flour
1 tsp. baking powder
1 tbs. butter

milk as needed
1 cup chopped
   peanuts, or
   other nuts

Heat oven to 350.° In a large bowl, stir flour and baking powder together. Add butter and enough milk to make a firm paste. Add nuts, turn out on a floured board and knead well. Roll into a ½-inch cylinder and cut into ½-inch slices. Place on a greased baking sheet at ½-inch intervals and bake for 20 minutes.

MACAWLY MACAROONS

¾ cup shelled almonds
1½ cups pine nuts
1 tbs. flour

¼ cup sugar
1 large egg white
½ cup raisins

Heat oven to 350.° With a food processor, grind almonds, ½ cup of the pine nuts and flour. Transfer to a bowl and stir in sugar. Add egg white and blend until dough forms a ball. Mix in raisins and remaining 1 cup pine nuts. Shape into ¾-inch balls, place on a foil-lined cookie sheet and flatten to ½-inch thick. Bake for about 15 minutes.

CHEESE CRISPIES

1 cup margarine
½ lb. sharp cheddar
   cheese, grated
2 cups flour

dash salt
dash cayenne pepper
dash Tabasco Sauce
2 cups Rice Krispies

Heat oven to 350.° In a large bowl, mix together margarine and cheese. Add flour, salt, cayenne and Tabasco and mix well. Add Rice Krispies and mix well. Roll into walnut-sized balls and flatten on an ungreased cookie sheet. Bake for 15 minutes.

BABY'S FAVORITE GRANOLA

¼ cup butter
¼ cup pasteurized honey
3 cups rough-cut oats
1½ tsp. cinnamon

2 cups mixed shelled
   almonds, pine nuts,
   Brazil nuts and shredded
   coconut
⅔ cup dried fruit (apples
   and/or raisins)

Heat oven to 350.° In a large oven-proof skillet or baking dish, melt butter and stir in honey. Add oats, mixed nuts and coconut and cinnamon.

Bake for 15 minutes, stirring several times. Remove from oven and stir in fruit. Cool completely. Store a 1-week supply in a jar with a tight-fitting lid. Refrigerate the rest.

POLLY'S BISCUITS

1½ cups hot water
1 cup uncooked
  oatmeal
⅓ cup butter
1 tsp. beef bouillon
  granules

¾ cup dry milk
  powder
½ cup cornmeal
1 egg, beaten
3½ cups whole
  wheat flour

Heat oven to 325.° In a large bowl, pour hot water over oatmeal, butter and bouillon. Let stand for about 5 minutes. Stir in powdered milk, cornmeal and egg. Add flour, ½ cup at a time, mixing well after each addition. Knead for 5 to 7 minutes, adding more flour if necessary to make a very stiff dough. Roll out on a floured board to ½-inch thickness and cut into shapes with cookie cutters (cat shapes are nice!). Bake for about 50 minutes. Cool and place on a wire rack to completely dry before storing. Makes about 1½ pounds.

HEAVENLY NUGGETS

¾ cup chopped nuts
8 graham cracker squares,
  crushed medium-fine
1½ cups peanut butter,
  smooth or chunky

2 cups raisins
1⅓ cups wheat germ
¼ cup honey
extra chopped nuts

In a large bowl, mix all ingredients together until blended and mixture holds together. Roll mixture into small balls and roll balls in extra chopped nuts.

SESAME STICKS

1½ cups whole
   wheat flour
¼ cup soy flour
¼ cup sesame seeds

¾ tsp. salt
⅓ cup vegetable oil
water as needed

Heat oven to 350.° Stir together flours, seeds and salt. Add oil and blend well. Add enough water to knead dough into a soft ball. Tear off pieces of dough and roll into stick shapes with palms. Place on an ungreased baking sheet and bake for 15 to 20 minutes until crisp and golden.

SEED NUT TREATS

1 cup milk
½ tsp. vanilla extract
½ tsp. cinnamon
1¼ cups honey
1 cup hulled sunflower
   seeds

1 cup sesame seeds
1 cup poppy seeds
1 cup walnuts, finely
   ground
1 cup almonds, finely
   ground

Heat oven to 325.° In a small bowl, mix together milk, vanilla, cinnamon and honey. In a large bowl, mix together seeds and ground nuts. Pour milk mixture into seeds and nuts and combine. Scoop out in rounded spoonfuls and pat down into cookie shapes on a lightly greased cookie sheet. Bake for 15 to 20 minutes.

APPLE CRANBERRY PIE

pastry for a 9–inch, 2–crust pie
¾ cup brown sugar
¼ cup sugar
⅓ cup all-purpose flour
1 tsp. cinnamon
4 cups pared, sliced tart apples
2 cups fresh or frozen cranberries
2 tbs. margarine

Heat oven to 400.°

Line a 9–inch glass pie plate with pastry. In a large bowl, combine sugars, flour and cinnamon. Add fruit and mix well. Turn into pastry-lined pie plate. Dot with margarine. Cover with pastry, crimp edges and cut slits in top crust to release steam. Bake for 40 minutes or until golden brown.

PARROTY PRETZELS

1 pkg. (10 oz.) refrigerated pizza dough
1 egg, beaten
1 tbs. water
sesame seeds and poppy seeds

Heat oven to 350.° Unroll pizza dough onto an 18-inch piece of lightly floured waxed paper. Roll dough into a 16-x-10-inch rectangle. Cut dough into ten 1-inch-wide strips.

To make pretzel shapes: Shape one strip of dough into a circle, overlapping about 4 inches from each end and leaving ends free. Taking one end of the dough in each hand, twist at the point where the dough overlaps. Carefully lift each end across to the edge of the circle opposite it. Tuck ends under to seal.

Repeat with remaining strips. Place pretzels 1 inch apart on an ungreased baking sheet.

Stir together egg and water. Brush pretzels with egg mixture. Sprinkle with sesame seeds and poppy seeds. Bake for 15 to 17 minutes or until golden.

INDEX